THE REAL READER'S

Slightly Foxed

'Taking the Plunge'

NO.6 SUMMER 2005

Publisher and co-editor Gail Pirkis
Co-editor Hazel Wood
Marketing Kathleen Smith
Publicity Stephanie Allen

Cover illustration by Ben McLaughlin

Ben McLaughlin was born in London in 1969, studied at Central St Martin's School of Art and has been exhibited for the past seven years by Wilson Stephens Fine Art. His work is in both private and corporate collections in Britain, Europe, the USA and the Far East. He has just completed a residency at the Albers Foundation in Connecticut, USA, and his next one-person show will be in New York in 2006. His paintings can be viewed on www.wilsonstephens.com

Original design by Octavius Murray
Layout by James Nunn

Colophon and tailpiece by David Eccles

Published by Slightly Foxed Limited
67 Dickinson Court
15 Brewhouse Yard
London ECIV 4JX
tel 020 7549 2121/2111
fax 0870 1991245
e-mail all@foxedquarterly.com
www.foxedquarterly.com

Annual subscription rates (4 issues)
UK £32; Europe £37; Rest of the World £42
Back issues are available on request.

ISBN 0-9548268-5-X
Printing and binding by Smith Settle, Otley

Contents

'I've mislaid my glasses', by Linda Leatherbarrow

From the Editors

It's a hopeful time of year. The stalwart London plane trees have unfurled their leaves, and the sun is rising higher behind the City domes, towers and spires that we can see from our now not-so-new office windows. City-dwellers are beginning, as Hardy said, to 'dream of the south and west', and we hope that the travellers among you, armchair and otherwise, will enjoy Barnaby Rogerson's piece on travel writing on p.11.

Recently, however, we attended a sad event – a wake for the Angel Bookshop, our well-loved local. Its owner, John Murray Brown, has been looking after the needs of Islington readers of all ages for several decades and has been one of our great supporters. We loved the shop's cosy and unhurried atmosphere, the carefully chosen selection of books, the willingness of John and his assistants to chase up any title on the increasingly antiquated microfiche, the determinedly low-key windows, their display cards, usually unsatisfactorily held up with Sellotape, sometimes slipping at crazy angles. No loud banners shouted at you, nothing pressured you to buy, but you never failed to come away with more books than you'd intended. With its position in the heart of Camden Passage the Angel Bookshop was an Islington institution – until the giants moved into the area and it could no longer compete.

The wake was attended by regular customers of all kinds who came to raise a glass and say farewell while books flew off the shelves at the Closing Down sale. As John said, 'If I'd been selling books at this rate, I'd still be in business.' An object lesson there – you don't know how much you'll miss your local bookshop until it's gone.

Another, more cheerful event for us was our appearance at the Oxford Literary Festival. About fifty people came, and virtually filled a pleasant wood-panelled room in the Oxford Union. The novelist Penelope Lively, who introduced us, began with a look at the history of small literary magazines, quoting Ian Hamilton who defined them in his book *The Little Magazines* as having 'small resources, small respect for the supposed mysteries of "how to run a business", and small appeal outside a very small minority of readers' – though she hastened to except *Slightly Foxed* from this description. In fact she joked that, with our rising subscription level, we are becoming 'dangerously mass market'.

As always it was a pleasure to meet subscribers, and also those for whom this was a first contact with *Slightly Foxed*. We felt great support and interest from questioners after we had described our experiences of setting up the quarterly, and what we hoped to achieve. And there was at least one other editor of a small magazine in the audience.

We shall be appearing next at the 'Ways with Words' Festival at Dartington Hall in Devon on Friday, 15 July, again introduced by Penelope, who will also be giving a talk on writing that day called 'Making It Up'. Dartington is a perfect place for a literary festival, a medieval manor house with a great hall, set in idyllic grounds, and well worth a visit in its own right. Details of Festival events are available on www.wayswithwords.co.uk.

We would love to see any of you there who can make it. And whether you are travelling to far-flung places this summer or simply staying at home, we hope you'll find this issue of *Slightly Foxed* good company.

GAIL PIRKIS

HAZEL WOOD

Taking the Plunge

SARAH ANDERSON

Swimming has always been my 'sport' and although most of the time it is lengths up and down the local pool, I always pack a swimsuit when I'm going away in the hope that some more exotic or exciting spot will materialize. It was therefore a real pleasure to discover a book that indulged my fantasies about swimming while giving me ideas for future watery exploits.

The notion of a long swim through Britain began in the pouring rain while Roger Deakin was swimming in his moat in Suffolk. The idea became an obsession and, inspired by John Cheever's short story 'The Swimmer', in which the hero Ned Merrill swims drunkenly home through a series of neighbours' pools, he embarked on a random journey to swimming spots throughout the British Isles.

Anything that contains water is fair game once Deakin has decided to swim in it, and the pleasure he gets from his swims is infectious: 'In water, all possibilities seemed infinitely extended . . . Free of the tyranny of gravity and the weight of the atmosphere, I found myself in the wide-eyed condition described by the Australian poet Les Murray when he said: "I am only interested in everything."'

From the fear of being 'poached for breakfast' by the members of the exclusive Houghton Fishing Club on the River Test, to swimming with a family who seem to more or less live in the Avon, diving out of their bedroom windows to enjoy a floating picnic lunch, to Jura where the water was 'gaspingly, shockingly, ridiculously cold', he

---

Roger Deakin, *Waterlog: A Swimmer's Journey through Britain* (1999)
Vintage · Pb · 368pp · £7.99 · ISBN 0099282550

is passionate about his swims. The temptation to strip off and jump into the nearest pool, river, lake or sea becomes almost irresistible. Water-cum-Jolly in Derbyshire 'seemed to embody in three words the very essence of the joys of swimming' – how could it fail? While at Gargrave, on the Leeds and Liverpool Canal, he resolutely plunged in, despite his fear of being sucked under a lock gate.

Of course there is nothing better than swimming naked whenever possible, as Deakin did in icy Welsh tarns. Indeed well into the nineteenth century swimming was always done in the buff, but now, when it has to be done almost as a rebellious activity, a naked swim can turn into something deliciously subversive.

Then, too, Deakin notes how a swimmer, his view only three inches above the surface, becomes almost invisible and sees aquatic life at its own level. He swims right up to a frog which eyes him unblinkingly, and he skulks among the reeds, unobserved by a party of birdwatchers.

Open-air swimming: the ultimate anti-depressant

Digressions into fiction, water-based stories and natural history flourish between lochs, pools and river-swims. Swimming with eels naturally leads him into describing their journey to the Sargasso Sea, a story I always find entrancing. He reflects too on Byron's Pool on the Cam at Grantchester, where the Romantic poet swam and where later Rupert Brooke, Rose Macaulay and Virginia Woolf bathed.

Sadly, that pool has now been made into a concrete weir, but Henry Williamson's *Tarka the Otter* territory in Devon remains unspoilt.

Some of Deakin's swims brought back memories of my own aquatic exploits. In a loch on Jura, Deakin 'returned across two hundred yards of the finest water in the world, tasting it at intervals. To feel its balmy softness in every limb, at every stroke, was a kind of heaven'. I too have drunk, from Lake Baikal – the world's deepest – after a day's trek through the Siberian taiga. It was icy cold even in August and deeply refreshing, though my companions were puzzled by this simple pleasure.

Some of Deakin's swims, however, would undoubtedly have left me terrified. I would never, for example, have braved Hell Gill gorge on the Yorkshire/Cumbria border where the torrent swept him along a steep and labyrinthine descent through 'a succession of cold baths'. His advice that by leaning into the water you can learn to respect it and should never fear it, would not, I suspect, have applied here. Nevertheless the adventure and danger involved in river and sea swimming are all part of the process of 'letting go' and making you aware of your body as the water that it mostly is.

Deakin is convinced that there is no anti-depressant to match swimming and manages to persuade us that he is right. In freezing water there is a heady rush of endorphins which the *Oxford Textbook of Medicine* says make one's mood change but which 'are difficult to validate scientifically, although feelings of well-being seem to occur'. With the exception of the proboscis monkey of Borneo we are the only primates that take to water for the joy of it, and we still have webbing between our thumb and forefinger.

The more Deakin swam the more convinced he became that our relationship to water is mystical. The ancients believed in the healing powers of water, and today the Ganges and Lourdes are just two examples of watery pilgrimage sites. But in Britain, though we have a tradition of sacred wells, we have turned water into a commodity – and that is unnatural. We should learn to value it. We also tend to treat it ignominiously. Architects in Japan, Morocco and Kashmir have used water for celebration and allowed it to play a prominent part in design, but in the Tesco car park in Bury St Edmunds the River Lark has been bundled into an undignified concrete canyon.

Deakin does not have much truck with indoor pools, but he finds outdoor pools exhilarating. 'If you tread on air on your way from the pool, it is because you are floating somewhere just above your corporeal self.' Water spots – lidos, pools, spas and the seaside – bring people together and create a community. Even London has exciting places in which to swim, such as the ponds on Hampstead Heath, the Lidos at Tooting Bec and Brockwell Park, the Oasis in Covent Garden and the Serpentine. Sadly, some open-air pools are now being closed, which is a shame. An outdoor pool is the perfect antidote to cramped urban living.

In the same way that Bruce Chatwin in *Songlines* uses an outward journey and its rhythms as a metaphor for internal mapping, so Deakin's aquatic progress is concerned with the geography of the mind. The rhythm of swimming is not only one of its principal pleasures but also its essence: 'Mind and body go off somewhere together in unselfconscious bliss, and the lengths seem to swim themselves.'

Deakin seems always to have used breaststroke so it's probably as well he didn't attempt his adventure in Australia, for as he says: 'You should understand that in Australia, swimming strokes are deeply gendered.' But regardless of what stroke you use or whether you swim alone or in company, to swim is to let your soul soar and your mind go free.

SARAH ANDERSON founded the Travel Bookshop in Notting Hill in 1979. After 25 years she has now 'retired' from the shop and has embarked on a gap year. She recently returned from Antarctica where she travelled with her bathing suit, but the opportunity to use it never arose.

After the Death of the Masters

BARNABY ROGERSON

Last summer the two masters of travel writing, Norman Lewis and Wilfrid Thesiger, died within a month of each other. As Britain buried the last of her explorers and the best of her travel writers, it became clear that a literary threshold had been crossed. The obituaries were unanimous in their praise of these great men, a pair of triumphant individualists who were born with a zeal to record a vanishing world.

Despite their passionate identification with different cultures and their public championing of endangered societies, they were both also self-effacingly modest. Indeed, by the standards of today's tabloids they might seem indecently reticent. Norman Lewis claimed he could walk into a room full of people and leave it some time afterwards without anyone realizing that he had been there. Wilfrid Thesiger could never claim such invisibility. His beak-like nose, craggy profile and taste for traditional tailoring, whether in Chelsea or Afghanistan, made him instantly recognizable, but his icy reserve kept him insulated from all but a handful of intimates. This self-discipline was not forced in either man. Rather it was an essential

---

Aidan Hartley, *The Zanzibar Chest* (2003) · Perennial · Pb · 320pp · £8.99 · ISBN 0006531210; Tobias Jones, *The Dark Heart of Italy* (2003) · Faber · Pb · 288pp · £7.99 · ISBN 0571205925; Ghada Karmi, *In Search of Fatima* (2002) · Verso · Pb · 452pp · £10 · ISBN 1859845614; John W. Kiser, *The Monks of Tibhirine* (2002) · St Martin's Press · Pb · 320pp · £10.99 · ISBN 0312302940; Deborah Scroggins, *Emma's War* (2003) · HarperCollins · Pb · 220pp · £7.99 · ISBN 0006551475

component of their role as travel writers. They were there to observe, to record the world dispassionately, not to paint self-portraits or to cast their shadow over the landscapes they loved.

This is not to suggest that travel writing should be considered a brood-sister to a scholarly work of anthropology. Although you may learn more about the nature of Neapolitan life from Lewis's masterpiece *Naples '44* and more about the realities of Bedouin existence from Thesiger's marvellous *Arabian Sands* than you would if you read a dozen academic textbooks, the reader should always be cautious. Thesiger travelled with youthful outcasts of Omani society whilst Lewis spent much of his time in Naples with prostitutes. Travel writing is always at its best when it is an individual's passionate response to a society. It seldom, if ever, aspires to a balanced viewpoint and is most famously effective when a whole culture is threatened with destruction. The writer can then pull out all the stops and indulge in a poignant elegy to a dying world.

It is one of the pleasures of a settled, comfortable life to indulge in this melancholy process of regret. It also helps prepare you for old age and death, if you can convince yourself that all the beauty of the world has been destroyed. However, if you have ever been privileged to witness the ecstatic delight of an isolated village at last being linked to the outside world, and given access to hospitals, schools and a market place, you might seriously doubt that anyone could resist such progress.

That said, the skilful evocation of a destroyed world can turn a travel book into a historical document. The young Mungo Park, his hat-band stuffed with notes, could never have known that with his diaries he was creating a prime source of West African history. Thesiger would also achieve this with his book on *The Marsh Arabs* (whose home in the flooded delta-land of Mesopotamia in southern Iraq was drained by Saddam Hussein). In *Voices of the Old Sea* Norman Lewis wrote one of the iconic books of the twentieth century. It chronicles a self-contained Spanish fishing village with a sophisticated oral culture of verse-making, just before it is destroyed by mass tourism; Lewis is almost completely absent from the narrative. This, I feel, is one of the marks of a true travel writer. The narrator's interest in 'otherness' is wholly absorbing.

Looking back at these masters and contemplating the present state of travel writing, one has to acknowledge that we are in a new era. Travel documentaries now record every corner of the world, yet they are a paradox. Travel, by its very nature, cannot easily be framed by a medium which requires, even at its most pared-down, a cameraman, a sound recorder, a director/producer and a narrator working to a script and a budgeted schedule. In practice, as the credits at the end of each programme so honestly reveal, the film crew will be much, much larger. As an experienced travel producer explained to me, one concept every half hour is all their target audience can be expected to absorb. A television audience will also expect an easy flippancy and will not normally tolerate more than ten minutes of filming in the same landscape before boredom sets in.

Such is the lucrative effect of the TV tie-in that anything with a whiff of television gets published, marketed and enthusiastically stocked by the bookshop chains. This is the world in which Michael Palin has become the best-known traveller of the day, his books selling by the hundreds of thousands. His recent work, *Sahara*, has been written in the form of a continuous diary. The reality was a series of country-by-country visits based on filming needs which involved the participants being ferried over for each session. For instance 'Day Fourteen: Tinfou to Tindouf' casually implies that Palin crossed the Moroccan Saharan frontier to visit the Polisario camp in Algeria. On a map they look close enough but it is in fact impossible to travel on the ground from one to the other, for this highly sensitive frontier with its unreported border war has been closed for thirty years. I like Palin better when he honestly records heading back to 'an English summer to cool off until the Saharan summer has burnt itself out'.

Travel writing has become an annex of the entertainment industry. Fellow-publishers have confided that sexual tension between travellers is always good for sales whilst a travel writer reticent about personal relationships will not help his book's 'profile'. Contemporary travel writers now skip lightly along the tracks first forged by the great explorers, ever conscious that with this trip they might finally 'break into' film. To add a sense of achievement modern travel writers will have to invent new ways in which to cross the Sahara or to trudge across the utmost poles, or burden themselves with a half-trained string of camels, an elephant, a fridge, a mule or an unresponsive girlfriend. In any one year you can be reasonably sure that British publishers will be producing a book touching on elephants in India, a horse-ride across Central Asia and a camel trek. By the end I am usually damp-eyed with concern for the animals and correspondingly irritated with the writer without having learned anything of interest about the humans encountered along the way.

So has the great British tradition of travel writing been overwhelmed by the combined effects of television and the new mass market? Who are the heirs of the great master travel writers? I called in on the handful of bookshops in London where the staff actively choose their stock. There are not many of these places left, but those that we have, such as Daunt's, John Sandoe, Heywood Hill and the Metropolitan Bookshop, have become as valuable as whole libraries.

The depression soon lifted. Even restricting my survey to the books that had been published in the last couple of years I found myself with an impressive shortlist which I have reluctantly whittled down to five. Looking at their spines, I feel an extraordinary new confidence in the genre.

I had already unwittingly met Ghada Karmi, the author of *In Search of Fatima*, when she spoke at an anti-war rally in Hyde Park, but her calm literary voice is a world removed from the fervent rhetoric of that day. She has also neatly reversed all the usual stereotypes of travel writing, for she is a woman, she is Arab, she comes from a Muslim culture and she is exploring England.

Though born in Jerusalem, her childhood was spent with embittered Palestinian exiles in a north London suburb – ironically also one of the chief Jewish neighbourhoods. This was the springboard for her passionate attachment to her adopted land and its tolerance. *In Search of Fatima* is the story of her love for England which is capped by her fairytale marriage to a liberal gentleman. Disenchantment and political radicalization ultimately follow, but the domestic focus of the first half of this book is a vital aspect of its success. For I believe that it is a conscious and skilful attempt to educate the British into an emotional sympathy with a Palestinian – any Palestinian – and so help break the hostile stereotypes that still dominate the collective imagination.

The Zanzibar Chest begins as a classic post-colonial journey of discovery as we follow its young author, Aidan Hartley, in the footsteps of his adventurous Empire-minded antecedents, especially his Odysseus-like father, who served as colonial officer, ranch-owner, agricultural adviser and finally as an aid-worker in his beloved Africa. Each successive decade of the late twentieth century saw such 'White Africans' ever more marginalized from the East African power structure. Aidan clearly sees his own career – he is a journalist writing on Africa – as one more step down this ladder away from any enriching involvement with the land.

To help understand this remorseless process of exclusion he also investigates the assassination of his father's best friend, Peter Davey, back in the days of the British-controlled Aden Protectorate. As the revelations of Davey's secret love affair with a Yemeni woman (and his secret conversion to Islam) are unearthed, so the tempo of Aidan's own life speeds up. His experience of the last months of the Ethiopian civil war and the implosion of state authority in Somalia, followed by the disastrous US intervention, creates a compelling, nervy and disturbing narrative. A chillingly competitive love affair with a fellow-journalist provides the right emotional setting for a final descent into the killing fields of Rwanda. Hartley has created a book fit to stand beside Conrad, Gide and Ryszard Kapuscinki's *The Shadow of the Sun*.

It also provides the perfect preparation for *Emma's War* by Deborah Scroggins. This is on one level an impeccably researched account of the short but tempestuous life of Emma McCune, an English aid-worker who fell in love with Riek Machar, one of the commanders of the southern Sudanese resistance to the Muslim north. It is also a very professional survey, and within the context of this personal tale, Scroggins neatly defines the rival ethnic and linguistic groups that make the Sudanese civil war such a complicated affair, without losing sight of the classic North-South divide.

But on another, much richer level this book is a dialogue between two different sorts of relationship with Sudanic Africa. For Atlanta-based Scroggins is also an aid-worker – clearly professional, well-briefed and efficient at her job – whilst Emma often comes across as a frivolous adventure-seeker looking for fulfilment and status in Africa that she could never find in her Yorkshire homeland. On the other hand, Emma was prepared to love Africa, to love individual Africans and to leave the privileged comforts of the aid-workers' barracks (and their Western-scale salaries) to live in a Sudanic village. While Emma ends up defending a tribal slaughter perpetrated by her husband, her ex-colleagues (there to feed the starving) go on strike when their regular supply of air-freighted meals is suspended. As a debate about the motivations of modern aid-workers the book is totally engrossing. Scroggins also has a journalist's eye for compelling detail, the kind that haunts the imagination and continually pricks the conscience.

If the British may feel ambivalent about their involvement in the Sudan, this is as nothing compared to the French relationship with North Africa. It is a truism of Algeria that the French are too interested, the rest of Europe is uninterested and so no one is disinterested. John Kiser's *The Monks of Tibhirine* is a beautiful, uplifting book that is all the more welcome because it breathes a spirit of heroism and courage into the scorched emotional landscape of French Algeria. Like *Emma's War*, it is another example of a highly professional work by an American journalist researching the life of a maverick European who dies tragically young in Africa. This recipe again makes for a compelling combination, because both Europeans and Algerians are assessed with equal weight whilst none of the tangled background of two centuries of murderous history is taken for granted. It is also a very particular book, in part because it is about sacrifice, in part because it studies the thought processes, rivalries and secret ambitions of a group of Trappist monks.

The story is centred on the character of Christian de Chergé, whose life was saved in the Algerian War of Independence by Mohammed, a young village policeman who stepped in front of this unarmed young French soldier to protect him from resistance fighters. Mohammed insisted that de Chergé was a good man and a friend to Muslims. The freedom fighters let them both go that day but a few days later Mohammed was found with his throat slit. Mohammed's self-sacrifice inspired the rest of de Chergé's life. Years later, he would become the dynamic head of a small Trappist monastery, energetically pursuing a religious dialogue with Islamists during the dangerous years of the Algerian civil war. The world needs such stories: of a Frenchman driven to follow the life of Christ to its ultimate conclusion by the self-sacrifice of a Muslim.

Although I learned a lot about Algerian politics from John Kiser, *The Dark Heart of Italy* by Tobias Jones is easily the most outwardly political book in this short list. It is a scorching analysis of Berlusconi's Italy and would be unreadable if one were not convinced that Tobias Jones adores Italy and fully intends to spend the rest of his life there. For only someone who is prepared to enter the political struggle should be allowed to pen such a biting, crushing, but also wickedly entertaining portrait of a nation state.

Nor is it just Italian politics and Italy's corrupt economy that are under review: even the Italians' football, their faith and the betrayed promise of their glorious cinematic culture are taken apart. Berlusconi is clearly the villain of the piece but Tobias Jones is too analytical not to see that he is a symptom, not the cause, of the country's troubles. Jones is also refreshingly different in not ascribing all Italy's problems to the lawless Mafia- and Camorra-ridden south. Instead he examines the prosperous northern cities – Milan and Genoa, with their so-called White Mafia, his beloved Red Padua and the deadly legacy of the unfinished civil war that was fought in the North between the partisans and the fascists. *The Dark Heart of Italy* will stand as a companion volume beside Peter Robb's *Midnight in Sicily*; another epic in the outside world's obsessive love-hate relationship with Italy.

The genius of a good travel writer is to take the reader by the hand and lead him gently, with wit and skill, into physical and mental landscapes he would never otherwise have encountered. As the world divides yet again into two armed camps, the need for observant travellers remains vital.

BARNABY ROGERSON helps run Eland Books with its list of sixty of the great works of travel literature. His own most recent book, *Heirs of the Prophet*, is to be published this year.

A Modest Superhero

CLARE MORRALL

I can't remember the moment when I decided to allow Biggles some space in my new novel, but I imagine he just turned up one day, demanding attention. An ingrained loyalty to past escapism meant that I had to take him seriously. There's an inner store in my mind, a bag of glittery details that I've accumulated over the years. Biggles was probably sitting waiting for the opportunity and jumped out when I was rummaging around for something else.

His presence in the novel has been the subject of intense debate with everyone who has read it in its embryonic state. How prominent a role should he have, or should he be there at all? Every time we discuss this in my writing group, we end up laughing. So, because I believe in humour, because I think it opens your mind, sets you up for suspension of disbelief, heightens your emotions, Biggles still has a walk-on part.

In fact, more people become excited by references to Biggles than I had anticipated. He evokes a nostalgia for a childhood world of heroes, goodies and baddies, right and wrong, that is immensely reassuring in these troubled times. Times were troubled then as well, of course, but you knew who the enemy was. He had a name, a nationality and a language – usually German.

Approximately 20 Biggles books are available as Red Fox paperbacks, at £4.99 each.

The first Biggles book – *The Camels Are Coming* – was written by Captain W. E. Johns in 1932. It was a collection of short stories based on the author's own experiences as a pilot during the First World War. He wasn't really a Captain, only a Flying Officer, but he thought the title would appeal to children. He and his protagonist, James Bigglesworth, were members of the Royal Flying Corps, which amalgamated with the Royal Naval Air Service in 1918 to become the Royal Air Force. Apparently, Biggles was the inspiration for hundreds of young men who applied to train as pilots during the Second World War, and many of the books were updated for that purpose. Camels became Spitfires. After that war, Biggles joined the Air Police and embarked on a whole new career as a detective. The scene was set for dozens of books with that heady combination of aeroplanes and adventure.

I'm not sure how the Biggles books found their way into our house, but they must have come from jumble sales or second-hand shops, or been passed on by other people. They had hard covers but had lost their dust jackets, and they were well-thumbed by the time they reached me. The ones I borrowed from the library were the same – they hadn't yet invented that useful see-through plastic that preserves dust covers for ever. I loved the ready-to-read smell of those thick, slightly yellowed pages, squashed up together on a library shelf.

I didn't care about, or even consider, any previous readers, but they must have been present in the musty aroma of the books, eager hands and the exhalation of thrilled breath leaving their mark. The covers were dark, usually blue, sometimes green or maroon, with plain black lettering: *Biggles Flies East; Biggles Goes to War; Biggles Fails to Return.* Oh, the heart-fluttering anticipation of that last one. Would he get hurt? Would he show some vulnerability – so much more moving

in an all-action, all-achieving hero?

Captain W. E. Johns was born in 1893 and died in 1968, halfway through *Biggles Does Some Homework*. There is some debate about how many Biggles books there are. Estimates range from 98 to 104, complicated by the fact that many stories first appeared in magazines and annuals, and were later compiled into volumes. (At the same time, he was producing plenty of other books. The Worralls series, for example, was about a member of the Women's Auxiliary Air Force, and was requested by the War Office as a recruiting incentive.) There can't be many authors with that kind of output. If Enid Blyton and Barbara Cartland head a list of prolific writers, Captain W. E. Johns isn't far behind.

My knowledge of First World War aircraft is extensive, because Johns provides detailed footnotes. There are accurate, first-hand descriptions of Sopwith Camels, Bristol Fighters, SE5s and all the other British and German aircraft in use at the time. The Camel had a reputation for being a difficult aircraft to fly, but it was the aeroplane flown by real heroes, the equivalent of the Spitfire in the next war. However, many of the books come from between the wars and later, when Biggles travels the world with his companions, Algy, Ginger and Bertie. They solve crimes, catch villains, save the planet from evil plots. Biggles is a kind of modest superhero. He has no magic powers, but he does have plenty of pluck and luck, and brains.

Ginger seems to have been Johns' favourite auxiliary character. Indeed, there were several times in the later books when I became irritated by his escapades, when what I really wanted to know was, is Biggles doing all right? The focus had shifted, and Biggles was no longer the slight, fair-haired, good-looking lad with deep-set hazel eyes that were never still. In the early books, people were concerned about him. I liked that. It meant I could be concerned too.

Of course, he couldn't go on being young for ever. Although he

doesn't age hugely in the later years, he has to be a bit more mature. He becomes an Air Commodore, for goodness' sake. You can't be pale and delicate with that kind of responsibility. I thought that Ginger had replaced Biggles in Johns' affection and I was jealous for Biggles. Ginger went on being the headstrong young man, brave, needing guidance, but capable of the occasional flash of inspiration.

Then there was Algy. He was significant in the early books, but he had to grow up a bit when Ginger arrived. He had a poor deal in the later books, assigned to stay behind at base, to phone the authorities, to be the back-up. Ginger had all the fun. The third of Biggles's companions was Bertie, who wore a monocle and said things like: 'Let's toddle along, old boy' – straight out of P. G. Wodehouse. He was only there for the humour. He never actually did anything. He's the one everyone remembers, however, because he is a stereotype, and people like stereotypes. You know where you are with them.

In my novel, where Biggles makes his appearance, I had most fun with the language. I have been to writing classes. I know all about style. You write: he said, she said, they said. Never: he averred, he opined, he expostulated. Johns doesn't seem to know this. '"Lucky!" ejaculated Biggles sarcastically.' Wonderful stuff. I wonder why these words exist if no one's allowed to use them. Is it fashion? Did it all change at some point, and I only found out twenty years ago? But Virginia Woolf and D. H. Lawrence don't use them, and they come from the same period. Who was right, them or Captain W. E. Johns?

Like me, Johns believes that humour is important. All the short stories from the First World War end with a light-hearted bit of banter to show that everyone would survive, that they weren't going to break under the pressure – the *MASH* principle on a rather more basic level.

Sadly, there are racial stereotypes which we would not tolerate today. The baddie is frequently a German, epitomized by Von Stalheim, Biggles's arch enemy, who crops up in the oddest places, long after the war. He leads a charmed life, like Moriarty, and always survives to come back in another book. But he and Biggles respect each other's cunning, brilliance of mind and strategic thinking. They never make the mistake of underestimating their enemy.

The air detectives often whizz off to exotic places – Borneo, China, South America and various mysterious Arab countries, where the Arabs are always baddies like the Germans. I'm not sure about the accuracy of the local habitat, but you need natives to grunt and use their muscles to do the dirty work. Some stories are set in Britain. I recently read one (in the interests of research) about a bull which disappeared and was found in a herd of cows, with white patches painted on to disguise it. I had the feeling this was written to fill in time during a few weeks in the summer while Johns planned Biggles's next great expedition to Outer Mongolia.

There are no women in the books. Nobody is married, has a girlfriend, or shows interest in anything female. There was an attempt in a First World War story – *Affaire de Coeur*, helpfully translated in a footnote – to depict an unhappy love affair between Biggles and a French spy, but it is very brief. She risks her life to tell him she has survived, and we never hear of her again. You can't help thinking that Johns felt he ought to make a gesture but that his heart wasn't in it. Who wants women in adventure stories? They just get in the way and scream all the time and want rescuing. And let's face it, Ginger is pretty good at needing to be rescued.

John Hamilton Ltd was the first publisher to produce Biggles, in 1932, followed by the Oxford University Press. From 1942 onwards, Hodder & Stoughton and Brockhampton Press seem to have

published Biggles books at the same time. Maybe they were coming so thick and fast it needed two publishers to handle them. They were also popular abroad. Biggles is twenty-ninth on the list of the most translated books in the world. Even the French (who, according to my sister in France, don't understand *Boys' Own* stuff) have accepted Biggles with enthusiasm. Red Fox have recently reprinted about twenty Biggles books, so they are available again for today's children – or maybe just for nostalgic adults.

There is still something pleasing about the simplicity of the stories in our cynical age – plenty of non-stop action with no worries about psychological damage or post-traumatic stress syndrome. There is no ambivalence. We know who should win, and we know that they will. Nothing is left in the air, as it were. Dated detective stories proliferate on the television and are hugely popular. People are nostalgic for a time that never was. Gentle escapism, and why not? There is no derring-do in Miss Marple or Poirot, of course, so perhaps Biggles is more in the Indiana Jones tradition – without the blood and gore. A cross between Miss Marple and Indiana Jones. James Bond without the sex. With a bit of *MASH* and Jeeves thrown in. That seems to sum it up.

Oh, and let's not forget the joy and romance of seeing a biplane taking to the air. In reality or in the imagination.

What more could you want?

CLARE MORRALL's next novel, *Natural Flights of the Human Mind*, is due out in January 2006. Her main success (until now her only success) has been *Astonishing Splashes of Colour*, which was shortlisted for the Man Booker Prize in 2003.

Feudal Afterglow

DERVLA MURPHY

It is peculiarly exciting to turn a page and find a strong personal emotion exactly distilled – an emotion hitherto believed to be one's private idiosyncrasy. Around the age of 13 most bookish children break into verse (the literary equivalent of acne) and I then wrote a 'poem' about corncrakes – specifically, what their crake did to me. (And continued to do until farming became agribusiness and the crake was heard no more.) On p. 282 of *Woodbrook* David Thomson says in a few words what I failed to say in several feverishly florid verses.

Woodbrook is a longish book yet everything is said, with graceful lucidity, in the minimum number of words. When Penguin put their edition in the 'autobiography' category, no doubt remembering how much bookshops and libraries value unambiguous labels, they oversimplified. In truth *Woodbrook* belongs to no category, for it is one of those multi-layered books that demonstrate a rare skill: how to ramble to and fro, apparently at random, between past and present, without confusing the reader.

In 1932 the 18-year-old David, an Oxford undergraduate reading history, arrived in the west of Ireland as summer tutor to the Kirkwoods' daughters, Phoebe aged 11 and Tony aged 5. Since the seventeenth century Kirkwoods had been living in Woodbrook House, between the small towns of Boyle and Carrick-on-Shannon in a corner of Connaught seldom visited by outsiders. By the 1920s

---

David Thomson, *Woodbrook* (1974)

Vintage · Pb · 332pp · £7.99 · ISBN 009935991X

they ranked as impoverished Anglo-Irish gentry, a wide step down the social ladder from their aristocratic neighbours. Somehow they were surviving on precarious horse-breeding and the Major's meagre Indian Army pension.

For generations the Kirkwoods had been Indian Army and almost inevitably Mrs Kirkwood was the daughter of an Indian Army colonel. David, too, had been born in India: 'My father and his friends could not afford the uniforms and accoutrements British Army officers had to buy nor the splendid life they were expected to lead with the help of a private income.' As a penniless youth, addicted to country life and without material ambition, David immediately felt at home amongst the Kirkwoods – hardworking yet impractical, warm-hearted, high-spirited, mildly eccentric and variously talented. The Major (Charlie) painted water-colours and spoke fluent Farsi, Arabic and Turkish. His wife Ivy was a gifted musician, and Phoebe was aiming for Trinity College Dublin.

Where I grew up, in West Waterford, Indian Army (Retd) families abounded and, looking back, it surprises me that the rural Irish were so aware of the precise social niche they occupied. We were puzzled and rather shocked by their heartlessness as parents. With varying levels of regret they sacrificed their children to the needs of the Raj, shipping them home to boarding-school aged 7 or less. Thereafter grandparents and/or uncles and aunts cared for them during the holidays. David Thomson enjoyed the countryside around his grandparents' home near Nairn, where he tried to learn Gaelic and toyed with Scottish nationalism. The year he was born – 1914 – one dear friend of mine, long since dead, was dispatched from Simla at the age of 4 to a Bognor Regis boarding-school and next met her parents in 1920. Ivy Kirkwood was left motherless at the age of 2 and met her father only twice, and then very briefly, during the next sixteen years. David scarcely mentions his parents and siblings – London-based by 1932 – but the fact that he made Woodbrook his home for ten years suggests a certain lack of mutual devotion. Or perhaps Phoebe sufficiently explains that choice – Phoebe combined with the Woodbrook way of life.

David soon fell in love with Phoebe – seven years his junior – and all those Woodbrook years were suffused by a love that had to be not hidden but controlled. An unhealthy relationship, we might say. Yet this book reminds us that the in-love state, before the promotion of sexual activity for its own sake had taken over the visual and audible world of the young, could be a significant out-of-bed experience, mingling suffering and exaltation. Throughout *Woodbrook* the David-Phoebe romance is a powerful and poignant motif, not overtly dominant but woven into the narrative like a golden thread, needing only occasional references to keep us aware of its wondrous importance.

Woodbrook House retained the afterglow of feudalism. The Kirkwoods' farm labourers and house servants had never been paid in cash until Ivy arrived, with her strange notion of spending money on peasants hitherto content to be well-fed, adequately clothed and sheltered, and presented with occasional generous gifts. Why give them a regular wage when the Kirkwoods themselves rarely had enough cash to pay bills promptly? To David, Ivy recounted a symbolic incident. In the 1920s, when Charlie's parents were still alive, a maid belatedly married, having served the Kirkwoods faithfully from the age of 14. Into her trousseau trunk went a Kirkwood dinner service and an ample supply of monogrammed linen. A few days later Woodbrook's Master and Mistress, honoured guests at the wedding feast, found themselves eating off their own crested plates. David explains: 'It did not occur to the bride to conceal what she had taken, and though the Kirkwoods were secretly startled and annoyed it would never have occurred to them to be so rude as to call attention to it.' To the locals that transfer of property would have seemed quite acceptable; Bridie had openly appropriated what she saw as a reasonable reward for years of unpaid labour.

When David first came to Ireland I was a baby, and many of

his descriptions resonate with my childhood memories: untarred roads, bicycles outnumbering cars by a thousand to one, the smell of carelessly trimmed oil-lamps, gleaming coal ranges and deep baths with feet like lions' paws, butter being churned, roofs leaking, horse and donkey carts tethered along the main street during Mass on Sundays, cattle, sheep and pigs taking over the town on fair days when taciturn 'mountainy' men in fraying greatcoats, their womenfolk wearing black woollen shawls and hobnailed boots, came down to the valley. And the Christmas box (whiskey, port, biscuits, chocolates) from the grocer who was paid annually – unlike the butcher and baker, whose accounts were settled on the last day of each month.

And then there were the rats, generating tales of hauntings as they carried potatoes upstairs to their attic nests. David only heard these frequent nocturnal bumpings as incompetently managed potatoes rolling down the stairs. I once witnessed this rodent enterprise by torchlight. Our rats nested behind the huge copper boiler in an airing-cupboard as big as the average modern bathroom. The rural Ireland of the 1930s was much closer to the 1830s (or even the 1730s) than to contemporary Ireland – newly rich, rather brash, subservient to foreign investors and frenziedly consumerist. David would not have appreciated contemporary Ireland. Yet he might have reflected that, given a choice of extremes, too much prosperity is preferable.

I can think of no other English writer who so clearly perceived the hidden emotional complexities of the Anglo-Irish/Irish relationship. During his first long vac at Woodbrook this history student came to realize how profoundly and permanently the Great Famine – an avoidable catastrophe – had changed Ireland. Eighty-five years previously the land around Woodbrook had supported thirty families, each cabin standing on its plot of two or three acres. In 1932 no trace remained of twenty-nine of those homesteads. The Maxwells and their four grown-up children, all employed by the Kirkwoods, lived in the only house still standing. Their great-grandparents had survived when all others in that little community had either died or been forced to emigrate. As the years passed, and the Maxwells' acceptance of David increased, conversations about Ireland's past reinforced his book-knowledge, making plain certain nuances that must forever elude the historian's pen.

I know how it works. In the summer of 1942, aged 10, I listened in awe to a neighbour, born in 1850, who as a 10-year-old had listened in awe to her grandfather recalling his adolescent terror during the Rebellion of 1798. To me that 92-year-old woman was history incarnate. In my schoolbook '98 was a remote and boring event, like St Patrick converting the Irish to Christianity in 432 and Strongbow intervening in 1170. Then suddenly I was linked to '98 at only one remove and it wasn't a bit like the history book said – gallant Irish patriots versus savage English soldiers. It had been a seriously confused mess: some Irish insurgents brave, some savage; some English soldiers savage, some compassionate. That unforgettable Sunday afternoon made me realize that essentially all history was about ordinary people and therefore could never be boring, however remote. It also implanted a healthy suspicion of history's possible abuse as propaganda.

When first published, in 1974, *Woodbrook* caused a few eddies of unease in Ireland. Northern Ireland was then in turmoil and many of David Thomson's readers wanted to look forward, not back. Centuries of animosity, of carefully tended grievances, formed part of the background to this new cycle of killing, maiming and intimidation. It seemed not the moment to recall those Elizabethan and Cromwellian campaigns so disturbingly brought to life in *Woodbrook*'s historical vignettes, made all the more harrowing by the author's penchant for understatement. In the reign of Queen Elizabeth I genocide was the name of the game; almost 400 years before that term was invented her officials advocated in writing and carefully planned the complete extermination of the Irish. When this attempted genocide failed for lack of funding, the Penal Laws were introduced: if you can't exterminate them all, demoralize the survivors. David Thomson is devastatingly shrewd in his analysis of exactly how demoralization worked – and didn't work.

Self-sufficient Woodbrook House lacked a wireless, and the *Irish Times* was delivered a day late, in the afternoon, by a cycling postman. Thus it came about that on 1 September 1939, as the Nazis invaded Poland, the Kirkwoods with David and the dogs were setting off in the back of a hired truck to spend three weeks holidaying in a primitive cabin on a tiny island off the Connemara coast. A few days later rumours of war reached them, but Kirkwoods don't panic and they stayed on their islet until 21 September.

David then went to London to be rejected by the army: too short-sighted and night-blind. Back in Woodbrook, he and the Kirkwoods tried to adapt to a new way of farming imposed by the Irish government's Compulsory Tillage Order. Most of the pastures and meadows had to be ploughed: Woodbrook's main economic prop was gone. In the very wet west of Ireland grazing stock flourishes but grain crops don't – especially wheat.

In fact the Kirkwoods' way of life was already doomed when David joined the family, and much of his book is a deeply affectionate yet rigorously unsentimental record of the last decade of a 250-year-old home. In 1942 the FOR SALE sign went up but no offer was made. David explains:

> I asked Tom [Maxwell] whether he knew what it was that in the end put every buyer off. He shrugged his shoulders. Then he said simply, 'Woodbrook belongs to us.' He said it naturally and quietly as though the whole world knew it, as though it would cause me no surprise. Of course I knew what he meant . . . His family were living there before Cromwell put the Kirkwoods on this land.

DERVLA MURPHY has written twenty books in the past forty years. Her latest, published in January, is *Through Siberia by Accident*.

Hoodwinkery and Legerdemain

MALCOLM GLUCK

The one thing that five of the six Stefan Zweig books currently in print in Britain have most strikingly in common is not the author's consistency of style but his photograph opposite the title page. The most famous of these, *The Royal Game*, notorious in European and American chess circles for decades, is the only one innocent of his image, the publisher preferring instead to show us a sketch of the battleground whereupon that so-called royal game is fought. The photograph in the other five books is warmly revealing. Herr Zweig's devilish Viennese smile – as evident yet as beautifully suppressed as a *maître d'*s as he spins a yarn to his richest and most despised customer that really, yes truly, there are no free tables tonight – underlines a polished French moustache which is given subtle uplift by the fourth finger of Zweig's right hand lying against his cheek. Posing thus he exudes the supremely confident air of a conjuror, a salesman of Hispano-Suizas, a hypnotherapist; definitely someone not to be trusted – and one cannot help but speculate on what his left hand is doing.

I think I know. It is writing the books. For Stefan Zweig is one of those sinister figures – an author who became British yet was for

---

Stefan Zweig, *The Royal Game* (1943) · 80pp · £8 · ISBN 1901285111; *Beware of Pity* (1939) · 372pp · £8.99 · ISBN 1901285499; *Casanova* (1928) · 96pp · £8.50 · ISBN 1901285189; *Twenty-four Hours in the Life of a Woman* (1931) · 112pp · £10 · ISBN 1901285480; *Confusion* (1927) · 96pp · £10 · ISBN 1901285227; *The Invisible Collection & Buchmendel* (1933/1929) · 96pp · £7.50 · ISBN 1901285006 · All Pushkin Press paperbacks

ever Viennese – who is supremely capable of the hoodwinkery and legerdemain involved in arranging his features for a photograph whilst cunningly carrying on scribbling as the photographer, concealed within his little black hood, explodes the flash. (The photograph was taken in Berlin before Zweig gave up writing Strauss libretti and fled the Nazis. He then lived in Bath before moving to Brazil with his second wife where he killed himself in 1942.)

Zweig must be approached cautiously. He can turn the unsuspecting reader into a recluse or a coffee-house wastrel. Some years ago I was due at a party at 7 p.m. Earlier that day I had come across a copy of *The Royal Game* and, unable to wait until the weekend, I opened a bottle of something crisp and Germanic and then the book and started in on both, thinking to relax for an hour before I left the house. When I next glanced at my watch, noting that it was uncommonly dark outside (and that somehow I had managed, perhaps in a trance, to turn on my reading light), I was shocked to discover I was three hours late and in no condition to party anywhere. The party-givers, being readers themselves, were most understanding when I rang the next day. But how could I explain I was detained by a book on chess?

In fact *The Royal Game* is not a book on chess (unless you are one of those people for whom Homer's *Odyssey* must be classed as travel literature). Chess is merely the psychological trigger for the story's vivid emotional premises. To reveal all of these, especially to tell you how the strange, and patently unqualified, individual on the luxury liner crossing the ocean to New York in pre-war Europe, manages to baffle the reigning world chess champion as they confront one another over a board, would be to spoil your fun. Perhaps it is better for the reader to have no interest in chess, certainly to have no idea how the pieces move; for the book deals, as does all Zweig's work, in the emotional and psychological friction created between people; their ambitions, their irreconcilable aspirations and, in the end, their startling humanity. The reader is left gasping, tugging down raised eyebrows, adjusting his values; if young he is awestruck at the chutzpah, if old (like me), amazed at the author's concentration and able to add the sheer silken pleasure of the read to that list of delights which includes one's first hearing of the *Goldberg Variations*, eating *foie gras*, or, in my case, falling in love with Lady Macbeth at the age of 10. An acquired taste, then, Zweig?

Well, he is uniquely *mittel*-European; part of that huge, magnificently sad and lonely hole left in European culture by the persecution and disappearance of the Jews. Is it not worth pointing out that had the Nazis, from 1933 on, laid waste to millions of acres of forests, polluted the reservoirs and rivers, destroyed all buildings above three storeys in height and generally set about gutting the heart of the country in which they had gained power, they would have been forcibly stopped? Stopped not only by their fellow Germans and Austrians but by a consortium of connected Europeans? Yet this is what they did to their culture in sociological terms and that is why talents like Zweig had no choice but to join a diaspora which, even today, seventy-two years after Hitler's accession to power, is Europe's irreparable loss. In reading Zweig, one sees the stylistic and imaginative literary genius that blossomed in Germany, Austria, Moravia, Slovakia, Hungary, Poland and other Jewish-touched cultures of central and eastern Europe (as well as parts of France, Spain and Italy). All now gone.

What is left are the books – in Zweig's case, books where the action takes place inside characters' heads rather than in conventional conversation or startling derring-do. Dialogue is often intensely internal. Yet one feverishly turns the pages as if gripped by what vulgarians call a thriller (as if life, for the reflective person, could be anything else).

Having finished *The Royal Game* I wanted to read more, and fortunately the Pushkin Press has satisfied my craving. I next embarked on *Beware of Pity*. In many ways it is Zweig's masterpiece; word for word the best value (and not just because it is 372 pages long, at a mere £8.99), paragraph for paragraph the most enthralling and historically detailed. It stands alongside other great books written about the same epoch (and with the same European cast of mind) – Robert Musil's *The Man Without Qualities*, most of Kafka, Hasek's *The Good Soldier Svejk*, the somnambulistic works of Hermann Broch, Joseph Roth's *The Radetzky March* and the astonishing Leo Perutz (several times bravely published in the UK by Harvill).

Beware of Pity is told in the first person and revolves around a single instance of the title's admonition. I cannot reveal this dramatic and simple incident precisely because it will mar your delight, or perhaps revulsion, but I can tell you it is immensely rich in the hideous and alarmingly anachronistic military mores with which the Austro-Hungarian army went to war in 1914. It is an indication of the author's casual genius that this momentous conflict is incidental, though the novel's protagonist does finally speculate on its horrors. Even so, all that pales into insignificance beside one single incident, in which the hero ignores the need to beware pity. He asks a woman to dance.

In fact it seems to me that all of Zweig's fiction – he was also a prolific author of monographs on such historically poignant figures as Marie Antoinette, Magellan, Tolstoy, Nietzsche, Erasmus, Balzac, Dickens, Mary Queen of Scots – has a distinguishing stylistic heart where a single, often banal, moment, like the beat of the butterfly's wings, precipitates a great drama, a hurricane elsewhere. Over that single moment the author worries like a dog with an intellectual bone; always chewing on it, returning to it, tossing it around, never leaving it be and never being bored by it (and, so, ergo, never tiring the reader).

Casanova, the one monograph of Zweig's published by the Pushkin

Press, is no less preoccupied by its theme, which Zweig does not have to work to establish, for we all know the principle preoccupation of its subject – the seduction of women. Instead of a biography we get what he subtitles *A Study in Self-Portraiture*. And that is what it is: a constant reworking, fascinating, hypnotic, as centrifugally devoted to its core as its subject was to bedding every woman he encountered, of the real truth of Casanova's life, his fears, his fearful secrets, his autodidactic personality and venality and victimization and creation of himself. Goodness, how I wish Zweig had lived to write a book like this on Freud or Kafka or even Hitler!

Twenty-four Hours in the Life of a Woman, beautifully rendered into English by Anthea Bell (who did Sebald a similar service with her transcription of his *Austerlitz*), is so intensely Viennese, though the action takes place wholly on the Côte d'Azur, that the smell of coffee and the aura of the coffee-house seem to be impregnated into the paper and the type. I say this because this edition is such a perfect size for the pocket, so companionable to take on the tube or, above all, bring along to the coffee shop. Again we have a story, told in the first person and compellingly centred around a simple incident which we are led up to and then away from. When the difficulties, the recriminations, the heartbreaks start, we find tears pricking the corners of our eyes and the cause is not tobacco smoke in the coffee-shop – for we have been careful to place ourselves in the non-smoking section of the place, or we are in a Starbucks which, say what you like about the company's distasteful American zeal, does not tolerate *der Raucher* on the premises – but the character's sheer humanity.

Once again Zweig works his magic: time becomes meaningless, the coffee grows cold, appointments are missed. You get to the end of the book and you resist the urge to begin again. But begin again you will; if not the same day or the morrow, then next week, when there is nothing on TV, no other book beckons, one's lovers are abroad, and the pub has long since lost its allure.

In *Confusion*, subtitled *The Private Papers of Privy Councillor R von D*, a successful man looks back on his life and, slowly, with all the skill of a raconteur, lets us into the deadly secret of his university mentor which so changed his life and made him what he is. Yes, of course, a woman is involved, of course there is the banality of a tragedy which is at bottom simply and intensely human; but this is Zweig, and so here we are again, with a story so able to touch our hearts, at the mercy of time which clocks cannot measure and inside an agenda we cannot control: we are glove puppets in the hands of the author and we willingly shed all our conventional devotions (except that of the devoted reader).

Finally, in *The Invisible Collection & Buchmendel*, we get two light, frothy novellas with a common theme: an obsessed eccentric of the sort who can only ever appear authentic in middle-European fiction.

The poet Blok said that the very sound of the word Pushkin made him feel exhilarated, and it must be said that the Press of the same name maintains this tradition. The sheer feel of the books, their design and smell, is delicious. They are a reader's delight. And in Stefan Zweig the Pushkin Press has rediscovered one of the ultimate readers' writers.

MALCOLM GLUCK, grandson of the Austrian Kaiser's barber, recently left the *Guardian*, where he was wine correspondent for more than 15 years. He has written two dozen books, is involved with a further seven over the next two years, and lives with three floors of other people's books and a bicycle in a notorious north London suburb.

A Positive View of Parasites

MICHELE HANSON

A parasite is often to be admired for its ingenuity and persistence, even if it isn't always attractive. A friend of mine once discovered a worm in his bed. It had come from his own body and had been living there for several months, beginning its tour in the previous March, when it manifested itself by giving him a cough and a bad chest. He found this out later when researching the life of the roundworm, which had apparently completed a convoluted journey round his interior, beginning in the spring. 'The female roundworm', he said proudly, 'lays a quarter of a million eggs a day!'

It is perhaps a good idea to take this sort of positive view of parasitism, because, according to W. H. McNeill, author of *Plagues and Peoples*, we are all parasites. 'Most human lives', he writes, 'are caught in a precarious equilibrium between the microparasitism of disease organisms and the macroparasitism of large-bodied predators, chief among which have been other human beings,' the sort involved in 'war, plunder, enslavement, tax farming'.

I particularly like the inclusion of tax farmers in the macroparasitic group. And now the bad news: humans are not a totally successful form of parasite. In the long run, we may be on the way out, because we have not ensured the survival of our host. Seen from McNeill's

---

William H. McNeill, *Plagues and Peoples* (1977)
Doubleday/Anchor Books · Hb · 365pp · £13.45 · ISBN 0385121229
Ian and Jennifer Glynn, *The Life and Death of Smallpox* (2004)
Profile Books · Pb · 278pp · £14.95 · ISBN 1861976089

point of view, up in God's position looking down at speck-persons, we have developed too fast and have made something of a cock-up of the ecological balance. The arrival of humans in the temperate regions, he says, was rather like the introduction of rabbits to Australia.

This is a horribly satisfying theory for those of us who already tend to the Swiftian view of humans, expressed in perhaps its most extreme form in *Gulliver's Travels* by the King of Brobdingnag, who describes humans as 'the most pernicious race of little odious vermin that nature ever suffered to crawl upon the surface of the earth'. 'From the point of view of other organisms,' suggests McNeill in an oddly comforting, matter-of-fact tone, 'humankind resembles an acute epidemic disease . . .'

'Hoorah! Serves us right!' I often shout out loud while reading, in a rather heavenly, self-flagellatory way, about the ghastly mess we have made of this planet. But oddly enough McNeill's revelations are not depressing. When one thinks of oneself as just one mini-particle of a greater mass, the self-blame diminishes a little. I am like an ant in a nest. I'm only obeying my instinct, which isn't anything like as bad as only obeying orders or acting upon my own beastly initiative.

Fortunately, not all of us are ghastly. In Ian and Jennifer Glynn's *The Life and Death of Smallpox*, some humans come across as rather admirable – people like Lady Mary Wortley Montagu and Edward Jenner who fought heroically to get rid of that appalling disease. Perhaps one needs to read these two books together – for the macro and micro view of humans. The Glynns provide those riveting little details that make one care again. Voltaire admired Catherine the Great for being inoculated while the French fussed and dithered: 'You have been inoculated with less fuss than a nun taking an enema.'

Not many parasites, as far as we know, can crack such jokes. And we are fairly unique in the parasite world, I would have thought, because we tend to have rows: about methods, causes and remedies, like the row between the 'vomit' men and the 'purging' men, and the inoculators (who used the smallpox/variola virus to create immunity, which made the subject contagious), and the vaccinators (from the Latin *vacca* meaning cow), who used cow-pox, which did not. It is things like this that I need to hang on to, so that I can go on being fond of my species.

But nasty is always more thrilling than nice and I am gripped by the horror of it all. According to McNeill, and I cannot help but believe him, we are nowhere near controlling microparasites. Or macroparasites, for that matter. Some people may think that because we managed to put paid to smallpox, we are winning. Think again, those people. New and more frightful diseases have burst out: Ebola, Aids, Haemorraghic and Lassa Fever for starters, all of which defy control. Only two summers ago an epidemic of polio broke out in Nigeria, threatening to spread across Central and West Africa, putting 74 million children at risk, and this week I see on the telly that the terrifying encephalitis lethargica is reappearing after an apparent disappearance of eighty years. It seems TB is on the rampage again too, but this time it's multi-drug-resistant. Those microparasites are still winning.

Keeping the microparasites at bay

What sort of a world would it have been without them? Without epidemic disease, apparently, Christianity might never have taken off. 'Care of the sick, even in times of pestilence was for [Christians] a recognised religious duty [and] quite elementary nursing will greatly reduce mortality . . . whereas pagans fled from the sick and heartlessly abandoned them,' writes McNeill. Gratitude and solidarity therefore flourished among Christians during epidemics, strengthening the faith.

Like Buddhism, Christianity also explained suffering. Both

started in crowded areas – Jerusalem and India – where there was more disease, and so it is little wonder, McNeill argues, that people coping with such 'horror and psychic shock' clung desperately to such philosophies. But he admits this is only speculation.

The more we travelled and traded, says McNeill, the better it was for microparasites. Travel meant fabulous conditions for the diffusion of infection. Caravans of traders, itinerant tax collectors and their accompanying soldiers created a 'bridge of human travellers'. The microparasites hitched a lift all along the Silk Road. They latched on to fur-traders, missionaries and soldiers in Canada, Buddhist missionaries entering Japan, pilgrims in India, slaves shipped from Africa to America; they hung on to beggars and nomads. 'Famines, migrations, concentrations and dispersals of human flotsam and jetsam, [all provided] fresh opportunities for epidemic disease to diminish populations.' Sea travel in particular provided tremendous opportunities. It was quicker, and travellers dispersing disease were stuck on the boat – until the next port; until, for example, all Mediterranean coastal cities were turned into 'a single disease pool'.

And if all that didn't spread death and disease efficiently enough, there was always biological warfare. In eighteenth-century North America blankets were sent out of the smallpox hospital to spread the disease among the Delaware Indians. A particularly vicious strain of smallpox that emerged in Moscow in 1959 prompted the Russians to collect it and cultivate it for possible future use, say the Glynns, in a rather terrifying finale. 'By the 1970s, a stockpile of 20 tons of the virus was being kept at Zagorsk – and 20 tons of plague bacillus kept at Kirov.' Some countries saw eradication as an opportunity. There is 'a depth of evil and hysteria in the thought that in the aftermath of a nuclear war smallpox should still be there to attack survivors'.

But 'Satan is not calling all the shots,' they say. I'm not sure about that. So I turn to McNeill, who doesn't bother much with good and evil, as he appears to believe that the spread of religion is all down to parasites, and provides, at last, a credible explanation for this phenomenon. Better still, those feeling truly, deeply let down by the Labour Party and their weedy version of socialism, can luxuriate in McNeill's definition of macroparasites. Imperial officers and private landowners, in his view, were the two social classes most directly parasitic upon Chinese peasant farmers. In the Ganges valley, cholera, malaria, dengue fever, kings, armies, landlords and administrators were all sapping the strength of poor labourers. What fun to see those macro- and micro-parasites all lumped together.

'In the context of the entire human venture upon earth . . . persistent population expansion is exceptional,' says McNeill. Our growth is probably due to some 'ecological upset permitting larger numbers of human beings to survive and multiply for a few generations until natural limits again assert themselves'. It's the word 'permitting' that grabs me. Why watch Hammer Horror? These books between them have it all: killer species, spillage from one lethal disease pool to another, creating havoc and destruction among virgin populations.

Those of us who watched telly in the Sixties may remember *The Quartermass Experiment*, in which a terrifying mass of experimental nasty substance grew and grew, swamping and killing everything in its path. It gave me nightmares for years, but McNeill and the Glynns show us *Quartermass* for real. We are living the nightmare, but at least we know why. McNeill explains, on a grand scale, everything that I always wanted to know about human nature.

MICHELE HANSON is getting on now and plans to devote a large part of the rest of her life to rescuing Boxer dogs. Dogs are considered to be one of the world's most successful forms of parasite. She is hoping to learn from their example.

On the Loose

MARY FLANAGAN

After my sophomore year at university, I took the $500 I had saved teaching swimming at the local playground and went to Europe, leaving behind the man I then thought I would marry. Michael had just graduated and, that summer, was doing social work among the street gangs of Manhattan's Upper West Side.

He wanted me to leave university for a year and travel with him in Mexico, a country he'd visited and loved. I couldn't or wouldn't decide and worried about my scholarship and what my parents would say. I'd also fallen in love, in advance, with Greece and was determined to go there. My future was a purposeful haze, and I probably thought that by excluding nothing I could have everything.

In August 1963 I was staying in Rome and running out of money. Then Michael's letter arrived. I stood on the pavement outside American Express and read it three times. He was coming to Italy. He had a cheap flight and would meet me in the Piazza Navona on 21 August at 6 p.m. From there we'd go to Greece. He loved me, this I knew. I also loved him. But I had turned 20 that May and was, as we used to say, 'on the loose' and wanting to be just that little bit looser if I could get away with it. I was escaping my upbringing (small town Irish-American Catholic), and I considered this mission almost but not quite accomplished. Michael was beautiful, he was sexy and he was good. I could not believe my luck. But it occurred to me that he might be re-entering the novel of my life a couple of chapters too soon.

James Baldwin, *Giovanni's Room* (1956)

Penguin · Pb · 176pp · £6.99 · ISBN 0141186356

To compensate for this structural flaw, I went to Athens and had the adventure I wanted to have. Then I nipped back to Rome, found a seedy *pensione* and holed up there until he arrived. For two days I lived on peaches and pasta and read James Baldwin's *Giovanni's Room*.

Baldwin's famous novel was published in 1956 when he was becoming not only America's foremost black homosexual writer but also a spokesman for the Civil Rights Movement. Baldwin outspokenly held white America accountable for the racism poisoning its society. He insisted that, because whites could not love themselves, they could not love their black brothers and sisters, and that they paid for their persecution 'by the lives they led'. Yet *Giovanni's Room* contains not a single black character. It is as if Baldwin is writing above race and gender in order to draw universal conclusions. The boldness of the enterprise still astonishes me.

Baldwin has been accused of indulging his homosexuality, then a crime in America though not in France where the book is set. But he always maintained that his novel was not about homosexuality but American loneliness and insecurity; about 'what happens to you if you're afraid to love anybody'.

David, the narrator, personifies the attitudes and failures of white Protestant America. Attractive, intelligent and well-enough off, he professes to have come to Paris, like so many others, to 'find himself'. At the same time, he will not permit anyone to know him. Baldwin, who lived for many years in Paris, was intimately acquainted with its gay, literary and Bohemian circles, and his evocation of the city's lush, enfolding atmosphere seeps into your pores.

David's fiancée, Hella, has gone to Spain to allow each of them time to consider their future. In her absence he follows his homosexual inclinations in company with two predatory older gay men, Jacques and Guillaume, meanwhile relying on money sent by his worried father. Through them he meets the dazzling Giovanni who tends bar in Guillaume's gay establishment. Giovanni fastens upon David who in turn is drawn to the beautiful dark Italian.

David moves into Giovanni's tiny chaotic room where, over the ensuing weeks, the tragedy of their relationship is enacted. Though he tells Giovanni of Hella's imminent return, he lives in a state of perpetual deferment, desiring Giovanni yet frightened and even repelled by the way he has touched his soul. Giovanni himself is a creature of light. Though hardly a saint he is authentic, with a sublime candour which Baldwin opposes to David's duplicity. His flaw is that he fails to protect himself. 'Look, look what you have done to me. Do you think you could have done this if I did not love you?'

According to his biographer, David Leeming, love is at the heart of Baldwin's philosophy. Love, for him, cannot be safe: 'It involves the risk of removal of the masks and taboos placed on us by society.'

Not even Hella's return can force a choice on David. Instead he casually abandons Giovanni, leaving him alone in the room without money or explanation. Resolved to preserve his masculinity, he seeks safety in Hella while concealing his affair with Giovanni. In fact he is incapable of loving either of them.

Out of dubious personal motives, Guillaume fires Giovanni who is shortly accused of his murder. Giovanni goes on the run, is arrested, charged and imprisoned. David's response is to flee with Hella to the South of France where the couple rent a house. Discovering she has bound herself to a man who can neither love nor make up his mind, Hella sensibly returns to America.

The novel is framed by David's last night in the house which will also be the last night of Giovanni's life. As Giovanni awaits the guillotine, David drinks away the anguished hours, re-reading Jacques's letter with its news of Giovanni's appalling fate, and remembering the loves he has betrayed.

Michael and I kept our rendezvous in the Piazza Navona. The next day we left for Greece, hitched rides with lorry drivers, slept in olive groves, boarded a boat in Piraeus and got off, by mistake, at the wrong island. I was happier than I ever imagined I could be. A week later Michael drowned in the Aegean.

I finished university, lived in New York, moved to London, became a writer. But my life is demarcated by the before and after of this event. The sharpness of its shadow has not been diffused by the years. *Giovanni's Room* was the last book I read before that calamitous journey, made at my instigation, and I wanted to read it again because of the personal significance of its story and a renewed interest in Baldwin himself.

It seems to me now both a fantasy and a morality play. I was surprised – and yet not – to discover that Baldwin worshipped at the shrine of Henry James. Both men are moralists, connoisseurs of the way we treat each other: their very words are moral, allowing for no excuses, no post-modern 'variousness'. What I had forgotten was the novel's political dimension.

How extraordinary are Giovanni's lines in the light of recent events. 'Time always sounds like a parade *chez vous*, a triumphant parade, like armies with banners entering a town. As though with enough time . . . and all that fearful energy and virtue you people have, everything will be settled, solved, put in its place. And when I say everything . . . I mean all the dreadful things like pain and death and love, in which you Americans do not believe.'

His words are a condemnation not only of David as the good white Protestant, but of the delusion of Manifest Destiny, America's crusade to clean up and sort out this dirty, disorganized world and establish an ultimate safety in which to pursue a fatal 'happiness'. For me the novel is prophetic, both about my life and my country: the waning of the Left and its failure to achieve social justice; the resurgence of the Christian Right with its mistrust of dissent and its eagerness to recriminalize homosexuality. *Giovanni's Room* remains a memorial to personal and political loss.

MARY FLANAGAN is a novelist and critic. An Irish-American living in London, she has published three novels and two collections of short stories, and is currently at work on a third. Her most recent book is *Adèle*.

Marxism and Cricket

PETER OBORNE

My most important ritual of the year comes at the start of April, when I burrow in cupboards and old boxes for my cricket kit. It is a harrowing process: this year my cricket bat has vanished, and it turns out that I have put on so much weight that I can no longer fit into my cricket trousers. This is an even bigger disaster than it seems because manufacturers appear to have given up making proper cream cricket whites. Sports shops like Lillywhites only offer repulsive stretch-nylon garments that feel as horrid against the skin as they are revolting to the eye.

Furthermore, this April was exceptionally cold and wet, so the cricket matches I had hoped to play were cancelled. I was forced to read about the game instead, but that too was a disappointment. It is frequently asserted that cricket has produced a great literature, but in truth no great writer has ever been inspired by the sport, in the way that Hemingway could be moved by bull-fighting or Tolstoy by hunting. Even P. G. Wodehouse only dealt seriously with cricket in his early school stories. Once he discovered his great comic gift he abandoned the game instantly, never to return. Cricket's most characteristic literary productions have been delightful but minor works: Hugh de Selincourt's *The Cricket Match* or the famous village contest in A. G. MacDonnell's *England, Their England.*

Only one masterpiece has ever been written about the game: *Beyond a Boundary*, by the intellectual and political agitator

---

C.L.R. James, *Beyond a Boundary* (1963)
Serpent's Tail · Pb · 288pp · £7.99 · ISBN 1852427329

C.L.R. James. It is a book that transcends all other books on the subject in the same way that Sir Donald Bradman existed in a solitary eminence above all other batsmen. I don't think that an English writer could ever have written a book of such calibre, because our literary culture has wrongly regarded sport as trivial. By contrast James treated cricket with deep moral seriousness, for in the West Indies, where he was born and bred, the game formed a central part of the culture of the islands. The most important theme of his book is how cricket created a new national consciousness which enabled the West Indies to shake off their colonial oppressors. The development of this argument confers a wonderful amplitude on *Beyond a Boundary*.

James had originally set out to be a Marxist intellectual. In the first thirty years of his career he wrote a treatise about West Indian self-government, a novel, a widely praised historical study of slave revolt in Haiti, and far too much laborious Trotskyite theory. He spent the middle years of his life, between the late 1930s and the 1950s, living in the United States where he unavailingly sought to bring about some kind of socialist revolution. This long period in his life has always struck me as a terrible waste. Based most of the time in New York, James was exiled from the game that he truly loved, and forced to follow cricket scores from the 'in brief' sections of local papers. It took the best part of two decades of this lonely, deracinated existence for him to work out that the American proletariat was not going to rise up in revolt against the capitalist system. It was only when he returned a disappointed man to the West Indies that, very much as an afterthought, he unveiled his masterpiece.

Beyond a Boundary closely resembles Cyril Connolly's *Enemies of Promise*, another solitary work of genius by a figure whose career was in other respects a disappointment. Both mix life and work, and contain long sections on early schooldays. The real theme of Connolly's book is how after Eton nothing remains to be done or achieved. *Enemies of Promise* is a brilliant book, but it is the product of a sophisticated, knowing and exhausted literary culture.

A large part of *Beyond a Boundary* deals with James's years at Queen's Royal College in Trinidad. The school's syllabus, system of discipline and house structure were laboriously modelled on the English public school and James, born in 1901, was a near contemporary of Connolly. But while Connolly allowed himself to be overwhelmed by Eton, James adhered to the values of his own upbringing. A scholarship boy, he was to be groomed to join the administrative class and rule the island on behalf of the British, but he describes with eloquence how other forces – English literature, cricket and the Puritanism of his lower-middle-class West Indian family – moulded him instead. 'Our bookseller was an itinerant who came once a fortnight carrying a huge pack on his shoulders. He heaved it off and spread his wares, the *Review of Reviews*, *Tit-Bits*, *Comic Cuts*, *The Strand Magazine*, *Pearson's Magazine*, sixpenny copies of the classics. "*The Pickwick Papers*," my father would say, taking up the book. "By Charles Dickens. A great book, my boy. Read it." And he would buy it.'

Unable to conform to the austere rectitude demanded by his West Indian version of an English public school, James broke away from school to play cricket, or to read, and he studied with enormous sympathy the leading players of his day, of whom the most notable was his close friend Learie Constantine. These great men walk on and off James's pages alongside Shakespeare, Dickens and Thackeray, and are expressions of the same indomitable spirit. Though James became one of the godfathers of the Black Power movement in the 1960s and 1970s, he remained steeped in literary culture. His admirable biographer Farrukh Dhondy recalls how he ridiculed then fashionable claims that English literature is a private matter for dead white males. For James the Western intellectual tradition was the salvation, and not the destruction, of black culture, and Shakespeare and Keats the expression of profound, civilizing values.

Beyond a Boundary is an exuberant celebration of everything that it touches. James uses all that he learned in his long life, his knowledge of Greek drama, modern aesthetic notions and theories of social organization, to analyse the game of cricket. This enabled him to produce passages which explain the game in a deeper way than anyone before or since:

> The batsman facing the ball does not merely represent his side. For that moment, to all intents and purposes, he is his side. The fundamental relation of the One and the Many, Individual and Social, Individual and Universal, leader and followers, representative and ranks, the part and the whole, is structurally imposed on the players of cricket.

No Englishman could ever have written a book as marvellous as this, just as, when James was writing it, no English cricketer could play with the freedom and elegance of the West Indian players. James just goes on producing his brilliant insights, remarking, for example, that W. G. Grace was as central to late Victorian culture as General Gordon or Cardinal Newman, and expressing regret that he had not been debunked by Lytton Strachey. This understanding of the centrality of sport is commonplace in the universities today, but it was heretical when James wrote his great book forty years ago. He produced the literary equivalent of the exquisite stroke play of Sobers, Weekes, Worrell and Walcott which dazzled the world as the West Indies came of age and the islands discovered their national identity. In Britain we have allowed second-raters to define our national sports. C.L.R. James's masterpiece shows how it should be done.

PETER OBORNE is Political Editor of the *Spectator*, and a fanatical amateur cricketer. His book *Basil D'Oliveira: Cricket and Conspiracy* was William Hill Sports Book of the Year 2004. His latest book, *The Rise of Political Lying*, is published by the Free Press.

Casting a Spell

COLIN MARTIN

Late one dark December afternoon in 1981, I came across a well-lit window in King Street, St James's, displaying the work of four artists associated with the Whittington Press, a private press named after its Cotswolds village location. Lured inside by this bait, I was soon hooked and the gallery landed two sales without difficulty.

One of my purchases that winter afternoon was the first issue of *Matrix*, a journal full of information about presses, type and type-casting, wood-engraving and printing. Reading it I soon realized how little I knew about what's involved in designing and printing fine books. Almost a quarter of a century on, I've developed a good eye for well-balanced illustration and text, and have derived a huge amount of pleasure from reading and collecting private press books. Graham Moss at the Incline Press has characterized the genre pithily, from the printer-publisher's perspective: 'The many shades of meaning contained in the term Private Press ought to boil down to a single common denominator: we publish what pleases us, rather than what pays.'

You need patience as well as cash to collect books published by contemporary presses. Years can elapse between ordering one from an enticingly worded prospectus and hearing the thud on the doormat that heralds its delivery. I'm impatient by nature, so I'm frustrated

---

Gaylord Schanilec, *Mayflies of the Driftless Region* (2005)
Midnight Paper Sales · Approx. 64pp
For further details see www.midnightpapersales.com

when books aren't published on time. However, the waiting always seems worth it in the end.

Given that we're talking in years, it is ironic that the book that stimulated this article deals with the most ephemeral entomological order, poetically described by Louis MacNeice as 'One only day of May alive beneath the sun'. The American artist Gaylord Schanilec is illustrating and writing *Mayflies of the Driftless Region*, which he plans to publish in the autumn of 2005 under his Midnight Paper Sales imprint.

Matrix has consistently championed Schanilec's work. I didn't take much notice of a brief note in *Matrix 8* regarding his book about the demolition of a river bridge at St Paul, Minneapolis, but its financial success enabled him to buy a small farm near Stockholm in western Wisconsin, three miles from the Mississippi river. In the first book produced there he captured the lives of four mid-Western farmers in interviews, their stories complemented with his double-page colour wood engravings of their properties. There was, however, no missing Schanilec's own account of this local history project when it appeared in *Matrix 10*, for it was accompanied by his striking illustration of a farm in south central Minnesota. From then on I was careful to pay attention whenever his name was mentioned. I also made a point of looking out for his work, but it wasn't until the mid-1990s that I bought a book from him – a Stockholm neighbour's account of renovating an old house, illustrated with colour wood engravings.

In collecting terms, I 'dated' MPS occasionally until 2004, when my relationship with the press changed to the bibliophilic equivalent of 'going steady'. I established a standing order, promising to buy a copy of every book published by the press in future. By this means printer-publishers secure a guaranteed income, and collectors get a discount on the books. MPS, however, has an even more ardent suitor, in the form of the University of Minnesota, which buys the press archives too, for its collection.

I first heard about Schanilec's mayfly project at the biennial Oxford

Fine Press Fair in November 2003 when he showed me a promotional broadside that he'd printed with his colour wood engraving of a species called *Ephemerella inermis*. Below, he'd printed a list of the structural characteristics that an entomologist would need in order to identify the species scientifically. It was a lovely paradox: replicating the delicate form and colours of the mayfly by engraving into hard, end grain blocks of maple wood. I decided on the spot that this was a project to watch.

Schanilec's interest in collecting and drawing mayflies stems from his passion for fly-fishing for trout. 'The mayfly, in a variety of species, is a favourite of trout, or at least of trout fishermen,' is his wry observation on the press website. 'Its emergence into the world is specific. For example, *Ephemerella subvaria*, or the Dark Hendrickson, begins hatching in early April, and is done by the middle of May. Furthermore, it generally hatches from one until four in the afternoon, and only on specific stretches of specific rivers.' Schanilec has approached the subject of mayflies in much the same way as he developed his book about farmers. Although he could hardly interview the insects he did the next best thing by consulting local anglers and Professor Clarke Garry, an entomologist at the University of Wisconsin who studies insect life in local trout streams. Schanilec then bought a microscope, specimen vials and preservative agents and set about learning techniques for collecting, preserving and documenting mayflies. After drawing a specimen he sends it to Garry, who provides him with a taxonomical description for the species. Their collaboration and Schanilec's use of scientific language in a 'fine press' context hark back to the eighteenth century, when similar collaborations between scientists and artists produced hefty botanical and zoological volumes of engraved plates of newly discovered plants and animals.

I've kept in regular contact with Schanilec by e-mail, providing encouragement. He's shrewd enough, however, to recognize that I'm also monitoring his progress in my impatience to get my hands on the book. He's familiar with such behaviour. In 2000, he printed a broadside with text by Bill Holm, a Minnesota poet and author. Holm admitted that he loved books 'as they might be loved by an illiterate sensualist. I love the bite of lead type on heavy rag paper, the sexy swirls of marbled endpapers, the gleam and velvety smoothness of Morocco calf . . . I feel my books. I run my hands over them as over skin or fur. I stroke them and sniff them . . .' I know what he means, though personally the look of a book matters more to me than its feel.

While Schanilec has been working hard, I've done some research too. My own fishing experience is limited. I have a half-inch scar on one fingertip as a permanent reminder of an Australian boyhood afternoon spent fishing for yabbies (freshwater crayfish) with country cousins, when I managed to tear my finger on a barbed-wire fence before we even reached the dam. The only skill required in 'yabbying' is to tie a piece of meat – preferably not from your own finger – on to a piece of line, drop it into a dam and then yank it out quickly when the crustacean's claws seize the bait. Another afternoon decades later, spent with Norwegian friends line-fishing from a motor boat in the Lofoten islands, also required minimal piscatorial skill. It seemed impossible not to haul in codfish. Of the skilled art of fly-fishing I knew nothing.

Help came from an unexpected source when I spotted an American exhibition catalogue in the bookshop at the Musée d'Orsay. *Casting a Spell: Winslow Homer, Artist and Angler* dealt with the nineteenth-century American artist's interest in fly-fishing and its influence on his work. Obviously Schanilec had stepped into Homer's rubber waders. Paul Scullery's chapter on the fly-fishing stories depicted in Homer's art provided a useful primer on fly casting. I learnt that it's an exercise in timing rather than strength. The angler tries to cast his line so that the dry fly, tied carefully to mimic a local species of mayfly, drops exactly in the right spot on the river's surface to tempt a feeding trout. Somehow, that basic principle had eluded me previously.

At first, Schanilec had simply referred to his continuing book project as 'Mayflies', but in the autumn of 2004 he added 'of the Driftless Region' to its title. This was another puzzle. Was he referring to stagnant areas of water? Searching the web for 'The Driftless Region' provided the correct, geological explanation. North-western Illinois, north-eastern Iowa, south-eastern Minnesota and south-western Wisconsin constitute a region that was not subject to glaciation during the most recent Ice Age. When the ice sheets that covered adjacent areas melted they left a deposit of rock and sand termed glacier drift. The Driftless Region is therefore named for its lack of glacier drift, a fact which is a source of local pride: one Wisconsin website exhorts browsers to 'Come take a journey through the land the Ice Age forgot!'

That same autumn Schanilec printed a keepsake promoting *Mayflies of the Driftless Region* for the annual Oak Knoll Book Fest in New Castle, Delaware. Although circumspect on details of the book's final form, the keepsake includes a fine colour wood engraving of an unidentified species from the *Baetis* genus of mayfly. Its structural delicacy and pale grey and lemon colouring are reminiscent of a sumptuous piece of art nouveau jewellery by Lalique. The book is likely to include Schanilec's colour wood engravings of thirteen species of mayfly with Garry's taxonomical identifications providing the core text. Schanilec will outline how his passion for fishing led him to mayflies and he's also considering interviewing Garry, whose enthusiasm for mayflies would enliven the text.

Then in October Schanilec advised: 'I have ten images in my hands, with one or two more available specimens in the hands of my professor (I've decided to cheat and use his if need be). So, things are looking up. I'm debating what to do about various editions, which is difficult as I'm trying to anticipate the possible fly fishermen and natural history book collectors who might be interested.' He may publish the book in three forms: a regular edition, of possibly 350 copies, consisting of wood engravings and text bound into a book; 26 copies with facsimiles of working materials and tied flies, the latter emulating the prized special edition of a late nineteenth-century book, Frederick M. Halford's *Dry Fly Entomology*, which included samples of dry flies; and perhaps 13 copies with an original drawing and the actual set of wood blocks for one of the images, along with other materials. Including blocks would certainly increase collectors' understanding of the printing process, although he warns that 'that would mean breaking up the archival materials, and I'll have to see what the U of M has to say about that, as they have had my complete archives up until now'.

Whatever the final form of *Mayflies of the Driftless Region*, its publication will be an artistic and literary coming of age for the Ephemeroptera order, giving the lie to MacNeice's lines, 'but the trouble with us mayflies / Is that we never have the chance to be grown up'.

COLIN MARTIN is an Australian freelance writer on art, based in London and the Cotswolds. He has a passion for well-illustrated contemporary private press books and spends more money on collecting them than his wife thinks prudent. Although she and their son would prefer a less dilapidated family car, she kindly suggested he read Louis MacNeice's poem 'Mayfly'.

Going West

ANNE SEBBA

I am next to a businessman at a formal dinner. The conversation dries up after the soup. At a loss, I ask what sort of books he enjoys. Risky, I know. Either he won't read, 'except on planes when I buy whatever I can find at the airport', or his answer will be as revealing as if I had asked him to tell me his life story. I am lucky. My businessman, more interested in fiction than foreign exchange, tells me, the book junkie, of a wonderful American author of whom I am ignorant. I am eternally grateful to him and still have the scrap of paper – menu on one side, 'Wallace Stegner, *Angle of Repose*', on the other – which I stuffed into my tiny bag.

Wallace Earle Stegner (1909-93) was the founder and for twenty-five years director of Stanford University's Creative Writing Program. Born in Iowa on his grandfather's farm, he spent his boyhood in Saskatchewan, Canada, and his youth in Salt Lake City. Author of many novels and short stories, Stegner was one of America's pre-eminent authors yet, as I discovered when I tried to buy one of his books, he is scarcely known in the UK.

Angle of Repose, winner of the 1972 Pulitzer Prize for Fiction and therefore the best known, is at one level a fat epic novel about the struggle to build America and the myriad forces that went into creating the American dream. The protagonists represent the opposing but equally strong qualities required to build a new country. Susan Burling is a refined artist, rather precious, for whom books and

---

Wallace Stegner, *Angle of Repose* (1971)

Penguin USA · Pb · 570pp · £10.50 · ISBN 014016930X

education are prized above all else. Often she appears to have more understanding of places than of people. She clings to the importance of an East Coast education for her son and the manners that she believes go with it. The unlikely man she marries, Oliver Ward, is a handsome engineer, determined to run prosperous mines, build crucial irrigation projects or own the patent to a cement-making process. He is the strong silent type, an adventurer who carries a pistol when he comes to propose, by nature obstinate or 'mulish', a characteristic emphasized in the face of his wife's superior education and sophistication.

Because Susan is an illustrator, it is through her eyes as she journeys bravely to her new life that we experience the dirt and dust, the heat and brutality of the emerging West. It is a place where men are hanged or beaten in what passes for rough justice, homes are as quickly pulled down as put up, and the demon drink is never far away. The shanty towns they stop at boast boarding-houses where it is assumed that Susan is a woman of easy virtue and she is offered only a curtained-off bed to sleep in.

Stegner does not have an idealized view of the West, yet some of his most lyrical writing lies in his descriptions of the towering mountain peaks and deep canyons, the satisfaction derived from creating a home out of the materials Nature left lying around, as well as the ever-present dangers of an untamed landscape. Above all, he brilliantly conveys the slow pace of nineteenth-century life, when letters may not arrive for months, if ever, or when a visit home takes a whole year.

But *Angle of Repose* is also much more than a book about how the West was won or how Native Americans were subdued and their land seized. Stegner, through his narrator Lyman Ward, is at pains to point out that writing a book about the history of the West is not what interests him. Ward, a retired historian now confined to his wheelchair as a result of a degenerative bone disease and unable to move his neck, is intent on chronicling the remarkable early life of his grandparents Susan and Oliver, whom he remembers only in their old age.

'What interests me', Lyman tells his disapproving son, 'is how two such unlike particles clung together and under what strains, rolling downhill into their future until they reached their angle of repose . . . that's where the meaning will be if I find any.' It's a clever device which lifts the book from being merely an impressive period novel to one with a timeless quality.

Lyman's sympathies appear to be squarely with Oliver, too trusting, honest and hard-working for his own good, who suffers a run of bad luck which drags down the whole family. Only in the final pages, when Susan is humbled beyond imagination, is one forced to reconsider the nature of the sacrifices she has made, imprisoned in her century as much as she is in her inarticulate husband's life, trying to overcome her hatred of the heartless mountains and the brutal West. As their fortunes decline, she is described as a woman 'dragged along after her husband's warped buggy wheels'. That she bears her pain until the age of 91, ashamed of herself for having been ashamed of her husband, only serves to underline her suffering.

And so, at the core, this is the story of a marriage, or perhaps the story of any marriage. Parallel with the discovery of the West, Lyman Ward discovers much about the desperate sadness of his grandparents' imperfect union, and at the same time he comes to understand his own newly failed marriage. Stegner shows huge compassion for Oliver and Susan's predicament and a deep understanding of how people behave in extremis, when 'I'm sorry' and 'I didn't mean it' cannot un-say and undo what has been said and done.

At the crux of Susan and Oliver's difficulties lies Oliver's sense of inferiority, sharpened by his failure to provide for his family and Susan's constant reminders that her commissions to write and draw for an East Coast publisher could see them through. Of course, we believe the version of events given by Lyman, this 'gorgon with stone lips', who takes his grandfather's side. After all, he's telling their story as well as his own. And he tells us that he himself has been cruelly treated by his wife who abandoned him after twenty-five years just when he needed her. Yet by the end, as a more nuanced picture of Susan develops, even he must admit some responsibility for his own marital break-up.

Rereading the book last year, I was struck by the clear-sighted forcefulness of the pioneers' determination to impose their will on a hostile and barren land; the desire to take a piece of wilderness and turn it into a home for civilization. It is a vein that runs deep in the American psyche but it may not be suitable for export to other lands and cultures – when I tried to order this book ten or so years ago I was met with 'Wallace who?' by a number of booksellers. Now, however, it is available on the Internet, as are other books by Stegner such as *Crossing to Safety*, equally powerful and thought-provoking, and *The Big Rock Candy Mountain*.

It is no coincidence that dreams feature heavily in the novel, which closes with an intensely realized dream sequence. Stegner understands the power of the American dream, and his enormous sympathy for those who have to settle for less than their dreams is what resonates long after the story itself has been read.

ANNE SEBBA starts her own epic novel at least twice a year, usually involving some attempt to understand her own grandparents' lives, one of whom trod the boards with an unknown Charles Chaplin. When not experimenting with fiction she has written five biographies including, most recently, *The Exiled Collector: William Bankes and the Making of an English Country House*.

When Ethel Met Sidney

FRANCES WOOD

I have always been interested in translations, for they can affect one nation's view of another. Thanks to Charles Dickens, Sherlock Holmes and a weepy film called *Waterloo Road*, for most Chinese, London remains eternally wreathed in fog, never mind the Clean Air Acts. And translation can ensure that books long forgotten in their native place continue to thrive elsewhere.

For me, one of the most extraordinary examples of lasting success abroad and oblivion at home is the 1897 thriller *The Gadfly*. Written by Ethel Lillian Voynich, it achieved a respectable success in England and America but became an enormous bestseller in Russia (first published in 1898, 5 million copies sold, in 65 editions) and then throughout the Communist world. It was dramatized by George Bernard Shaw and filmed twice in Russia, the second time with a score written by Shostakovich. Fiercely anti-clerical, sometimes overly theological, it nevertheless cracks along like an Errol Flynn film.

The story begins sedately in a theological seminary in Pisa in 1833 where Arthur, a young Englishman, is sorting out Canon Montanelli's papers. The Canon addresses Arthur as 'Dear little one' and puts his hand on the boy's shoulder rather too often for this twenty-first-century reader. Arthur, from a British shipping family long established in Leghorn, is a troubled soul, distressed by the recent death of his

---

There have been several paperback reissues of *The Gadfly* in the past thirty years but none now appears to be in print. However, copies can be obtained through second-hand bookshops or the Internet.

sad, widowed mother, estranged from his older stepbrothers, and wondering whether he should join the illegal political movement called Young Italy.

Arthur is also suffering from unrequited love for Jim (real name Jennifer) a childhood playmate, who has another suitor, Giovanni Bolla, a fellow-member of Young Italy. Jim is determined that violent struggle is the only way forward; Arthur is more uncertain, and his confusion between religion and politics, love and jealousy, leads him to bare his soul with dangerous candour in the confessional. Father Cardi, a slippery prelate, betrays his secrets, and various members of Young Italy are arrested. When Arthur is released, his stepbrother reveals the fact that Canon Montanelli is Arthur's real father, which is an unwelcome discovery for Arthur but at least explains the endearments. Distraught at this news and at the fact that Jim believes he has betrayed his comrades, Arthur slips out of Leghorn and makes for South America.

Part two opens in Florence, twenty years later. Jim, who thinks that Arthur has drowned himself because she accused him of betrayal, is now a widow, but she continues her revolutionary activities as Church, State and Young Italy vie for power. All Florence is talking about a mysterious revolutionary Brazilian called Felice Rivarez, nicknamed 'the Gadfly', who has come to join the fight. His physical courage is legendary but his nickname derives from the sharp and witty political skits he publishes. He is rather a bundle of attributes: 'right foot lame; left arm twisted; two fingers missing on left hand; recent sabre-cut across face; stammers'. He has arrived in Italy with a dancer called Zita whom he seems to have rescued from a brothel but who feels hard done by because he does not love her. The Gadfly's rather disciplinarian approach to Zita is contrasted with his extremely gentle treatment of a tiny, frozen, starving child he finds in the street. As Zita doesn't want a dirty urchin in her lodgings, he takes the infant to Jim's house.

The alert reader will by now suspect that the Gadfly is in fact

Arthur, but Jim is maddeningly obtuse. She and the Gadfly have long flirtatious conversations in which he describes his sufferings in Brazil as a docker, brothel bouncer and clown. Their almost endless circling is paralleled by the Gadfly's stalking of Canon (now Cardinal) Montanelli, who has been expiating his sins by flirting with the cause of the people. The final climax comes when the Gadfly is captured (sacrificing himself to enable his friends to escape) and Montanelli tries to prevent his execution. The Gadfly, his stammer mysteriously cured, shouts at his father,

> Come out of this plague-stricken Church – come away with us into the light . . . Padre, the dawn is close upon us – will you miss your part in the sunrise? Wake up, and let us forget the horrible nightmares – wake up and we will begin our life again!

The Gadfly dies in a welter of bullets, pushing a bloodstained crucifix from him; Jim weeps buckets; and the Cardinal dies of a broken heart – 'Aneurism is as good a word as any other' – having dashed the Host from the altar.

Knowing vaguely of its success and continuing significance in Communist China, I was delighted to acquire my first copy of *The Gadfly*, an English-language paperback published in Shanghai in 1986, with synopsis and notes in Chinese. It was lying on a table in the Guanghwa bookshop in Newport Place. It was a bit dog-eared and I now realize with guilt, though it is much too late to do anything about it, that the charming old shop assistant Mr Chen had probably been in the middle of reading it when I bought it. As well as its acceptable revolutionary content, the novel contains rather a lot of theology, and so notes were clearly essential for Chinese readers, though they are not always quite up to scratch. I am especially fond of the translation into Chinese of *Ave Maria, Regina Coeli*, which reads 'Goodbye Maria, Queen of the Heavenly Kingdom'.

Ethel: an unlikely life

I acquired a second copy in the wonderful second-hand and antiquarian bookshop in Highgate, Fisher and Sperr. It is a gaudy 1973 Pan paperback with a gun and a rose on the cover and a plug from Bertrand Russell near the end of his very long life: 'The most exciting novel I have ever read in the English language'. One wonders if he read much fiction. Despite its cover, the Pan edition contains quite a lot of information about its author which I found extraordinary, for her life was even more unlikely than the events in her novel.

Ethel Lillian Voynich was born in Cork, in 1864, the fourth daughter of George and Mary Everest Boole. George, who died in the year Ethel was born, was the son of a shoemaker and became a brilliant mathematician and logician, the creator of Boolean logic which lies behind the design of modern computers. His wife, Mary Everest (niece of the Surveyor of India after whom the mountain was named), was a woman of strongly held but eccentric views. Some suggest that her personal version of homeopathy may have hastened her husband's early death. He arrived home soaking wet and suffering from a cold. Believing that the cure should resemble the complaint, Mary poured buckets of water over him until he developed pneumonia.

Described as 'A Teacher of Brain Liberation', Mary supported the family by writing books on an astonishing range of subjects. They included *The Forging of Passion into Power*, *Miss Education and Her Garden: A Short Summary of the Educational Blunders of Half a Century*, *Philosophy and Fun of Algebra*, *The Message of Psychic Science to Mothers and Nurses*, an introduction to *The Value of a Maimed Life* and *What One Might Say to a Schoolboy.*

Her daughter Ethel was clearly attracted to revolutionaries and in a Gothick gesture apparently wore black until the day she married, 'to mourn the state of the world'. Significantly for her novel, one of her early heroes was the Italian revolutionary Giuseppe Mazzini whom she worshipped for his 'melancholy beauty and distinction'. She became interested in Russia and, through her friend Charlotte Wilson (mistress of Prince Kropotkin), started language lessons in London with the exiled revolutionary and assassin Stepniak (Sergei Mikhailovich Kravchinsky) who had fled Russia in 1884. Despite his low brow, bristly beard and fierce wife Fanny, he seems to have charmed many left-leaning ladies, including the noted translator of Turgenev, Constance Garnett, and her sister-in-law Olive. In 1887, Ethel left for St Petersburg where she stayed with Stepniak's revolutionary relations and gave lessons in English and music. She returned to London two years later and in 1892 married a friend of Stepniak's, the Polish revolutionary Wilfred Voynich. Voynich had been imprisoned for political activities in Siberia and had fled to England in 1890 where, while continuing to work underground for the Society of Friends of Russian Freedom, he became a respected and successful antiquarian bookseller.

Just as George Boole is now remembered for Boolean logic, so Voynich is still remembered, more than sixty years after his death, for the 'Voynich manuscript', otherwise known as 'the most mysterious manuscript in the world' and now in the Bienecke Library at Yale. Discovered by Voynich in the Jesuit College at the Villa Mondragone in 1912, the late medieval manuscript includes drawings of plants, pictures of women in 'bathtubs connected by intricate plumbing' and 'tiny naked people in rubbish bins', accompanied by a text in a script which has still not been deciphered.

The Voynich marriage seems to have been a happy one and to have survived Ethel's rumoured affair with Sidney Reilly, the 'Ace of Spies', who was said to possess 'eleven passports and a wife to go with each'. Sidney Reilly was born Sigmund Georgevich Rosenblum, probably in Odessa, but he was not to become famous until 1918 when he marched into the Kremlin, claiming he had been sent by Lloyd George to find out exactly what the Bolsheviks' aims and intentions were. (Reilly was eventually murdered by the Bolsheviks in 1925.)

According to Bruce Lockhart, the British consul in Moscow, Reilly accompanied Ethel to Italy in 1895, probably on a clandestine mission for the Friends of Russian Freedom and in defiance of conventional morality, for they were not married and he was ten years younger than she. In Italy, according to the afterword in the Pan edition of *The Gadfly*, 'under the Mediterranean sun and under the influence of the Roman Catholic Church which touched every facet of Italian life', Reilly revealed some details of his early life to Ethel. He claimed that a Viennese doctor who had befriended him was in fact his real father (shades of Montanelli). He had also apparently spent some years in Brazil, working on a plantation and as a docker, a clown in the circus and a doorman in a brothel (all of which, of course, form part of Arthur/Felice Rivarez's CV).

How much of this was true is hard to say. Reilly was only about 22 when he was supposed to have confided in Ethel and it seems unlikely he could have packed in so much by then. Since he was later to claim as many identities as he had passports, it is difficult to know what, if anything, he directly contributed to *The Gadfly*. What is more likely is that he borrowed from the novel when telling his 'life story' to Bruce Lockhart in Moscow in 1918. Ethel herself claimed that Jim/Jennifer was 'the only person in *The Gadfly* I took more or less from life' and that she was based on her friend Charlotte Wilson. If Sidney Reilly really was the model for the Gadfly, his subsequent murder by the Bolsheviks, no doubt keen readers of the novel in translation, was tragically ironic.

At the beginning of the First World War, Voynich moved his antiquarian book business from 68 Shaftesbury Avenue to New York, where he died in 1930. Ethel eventually joined him there. She wrote several more novels, none of which achieved the same success as *The Gadfly*, but no one seems to have taken much notice of her. In a country gripped by McCarthyism, her popularity in Soviet Russia and Communist China cannot have been particularly helpful to her, and presumably her royalties were frozen in Soviet bank accounts. She died in New York in 1960.

From Boolean logic to the Ace of Spies and millions of Chinese wondering what on earth the Church of Rome was up to, I find the details of her life fascinating. Yet if you look in any dictionary of famous women, there is no one between Mrs Karl Marx (née Von Trotha) and Diana Vreeland.

That, however, is not the end of an extraordinary story. Ethel Voynich is listed in the American National Union Catalog, where you will find a number of her works dated to the 1940s and held in the New York Public Library. These are not books but, amazingly, musical scores. They include 'Epitaph in ballad form: cantata for male choir and orchestra: In memoriam Roger David Casement, Brixton Prison' and 'The Submerged City: cantata for solo baritone, mixed choir and orchestra'.

FRANCES WOOD is lucky to work in the British Library, where pursuing Ethel Voynich's life was made easier by access to her mother's books, her novels, articles in *History Today*, a Russian biography and the assistance of Chris Thomas of the Slavonic section.

On Matters Mekong

JOHN KEAY

Scrolling idly through the SOAS Library's subject catalogue, I must have brushed an unusual combination of keys, so activating a random function not mentioned on the options bar nor widely known to researchers. The feat has since proved impossible to repeat. But I keep trying; for it was thanks to this truly serendipitous action that up flashed a title which, for its crystal candour, can seldom have been bettered. *Fish and Fish Dishes of Laos* was so specific it had to be just that – a handbook and culinary guide to the fish to be found in landlocked Laos. The author was Alan Davidson, the publisher Prospect Books, the category 'Long Loan', and the status 'Available'. Like a minnow into the reeds, I darted to the stacks.

There are not many books on Laos. If that is your subject area, you soon become familiar with most of them and hanker after other company. I had already gutted the histories, trudged through the forest with the travellers, taken a turn among the hill tribes with the social anthropologists, and become entangled in the government's statistical reports. Fish, though, were something different. A whole book on the fish of a country whose natural history has largely escaped scientific scrutiny and which possesses neither a fishing fleet nor a coastline was worth inspection.

Alan Davidson, *Fish and Fish Dishes of Laos* (1975)
Prospect Books · Pb · 208pp · £15 · ISBN 0907325955
A Kipper with My Tea: Selected Essays on Food (1989) is now out of print but Prospect Books (Allaleigh House, Blackawton, Totnes, Devon TQ9 7DL: www.prospectbooks.co.uk) have a few copies left.

Whatever the merits of the book itself, I was intrigued by its genesis. I wondered, for instance, what could have recommended the subject to the presumably non-Lao Davidson; who had he supposed would read such a work; and with the prospect of only a minimal sale, what on earth had prompted Prospect Books of Totnes to publish it? The SOAS copy ran to about 200 pages, one per fish, each with a line drawing. It hadn't been out on loan for eight years. Perhaps it was the only copy in existence. I cushioned it in my backpack and headed home for a leisurely appraisal.

There then began a process of revelation and acquaintance so rewarding that I now feel no shame at all in confessing my prior ignorance of Davidson and all his great works. In fact I pity those for whom Alan Davidson is a household name. They will never know the delight of a chance encounter on matters Mekong courtesy of the SOAS catalogue, nor the even greater pleasure of discovering an exceptionally beguiling writer in such otherwise undistinguished company. Only the random thoughts to which that catalogue encounter gave rise may strike a chord, for they concern the reader-author relationship.

'Oh, so you're reading Davidson,' said a friend.

'Yes, he's very good on the Giant Mekong Catfish.'

'But have you read the catfish piece in *A Kipper for My Tea*?'

I hadn't; so I got that too. The Giant Mekong Catfish surfaces in quite a few of Davidson's books, most of which have nothing to do with Laos or the Mekong. Evidently he felt drawn to this shy creature. To anyone obsessed by the wildest of Asia's rivers (him in the 1970s, me in the 1990s), the fish assumes a prominence wildly out of proportion to its elusive reputation. Indeed, proportion is much the most notable of its few known characteristics. Specimens of over 250 kilos have been recorded; of the one described by Davidson the head alone weighed 49.5 kilos. It is probably the largest freshwater fish in the world.

In *Fish and Fish Dishes of Laos* other finny curiosities are no less lovingly described. There's a perch that climbs trees, a carp that feeds on grass cuttings, an archerfish that fires high-velocity water-bullets, and a lesser catfish that goes walkabout down dusty Lao lanes, usually alone and always at night. It belongs, like other common catfish, to the Latin genus *Pangasius.* Only the Giant Mekong Catfish is a *Pangasianodon*, which led me to suppose that it might be descended from a dinosaur and have some Jurassic affinity with, say, the iguanadon or the mastodon. I was of course hopelessly wrong. The added-on '*-anodon*' simply means 'toothless'. For all its girth and its two-to-three-metre length, *Pangasianodon gigas* is the gentlest of giants and would harm you only if it fell on you. It is thought to feed entirely on algae, to frequent the river's depths (over a hundred

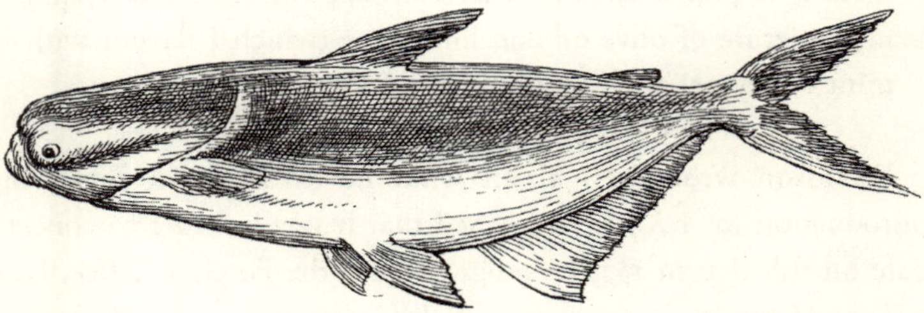

The gentlest of giants

metres in places), and to migrate for spawning; no one knows where or when, nor whether a breeding population still exists.

Obviously its endangered status troubled Davidson. In *A Kipper with My Tea* he admitted to having once joined a Lao fishing party. This proved to be a highly ritualized affair requiring a suitable phase of the moon, elaborate offerings to numerous spirits, and some prior abstinence from such things as sex and alcohol. Even when actually fishing, the anglers had to observe a rubric to the effect that they keep up a constant stream of verbal abuse. 'They had to call each other "bald-headed fool" and other even more uncomplimentary names,' says Davidson, 'and they exchanged sexual insults in the most liberal manner.' Despite this – or because of it – 'they did catch some'; but as to what became of the catch Davidson says nothing.

Only in the earlier book, with its promise of dishes as well as fishes, had the culinary aspect been covered. Diffidently and with just a hint of one-up-manship, he there revealed that he had both cooked and eaten it, and could confirm its near-legendary distinction. The flesh was 'of superlative quality . . . admirable texture and unmatched flavour'. Like the sturgeon, it bore some resemblance to veal, and 'there are those', he continued, 'who, tasting it for the first time, insist that it must be meat rather than fish'.

> Yet it is fishy, in a subtle and majestic way. Thin escalopes may be deep-fried or pan-fried successfully. But I think the best treatment is to grill steaks over charcoal, dipping them beforehand in a mixture of olive oil and lime juice (which I flavour with mint or thyme) and basting them during the cooking . . .

Davidson wrote best about what he loved most. From the Introduction to *A Kipper*, I learned that it was in order to concentrate on fish that in 1975 he resigned from the Foreign Office. Laos had thus been his last ambassadorial posting and, with a neat symmetry, he was Her Britannic Majesty's last ambassador there; for as the Pathet Lao cadres tightened their grip on the country, British representation was withdrawn and has yet to be restored.

For Laos, communism led to isolation, and for Davidson fish led to seafood. Penguin had published his *Mediterranean Seafood* in 1972, following an earlier diplomatic posting to Tunis. Other now classic volumes – *Seafood of the North Atlantic*, *Seafood of South East Asia* – followed. These led on to food in general. A small industry of publications and symposia, all devoted to the adumbration of neglected culinary classics and unlikely cuisines, resulted. Although most of his own books were first published by more mainstream houses, Prospect Books was another Davidson creation; so was *Petit Propos Culinaires*, its 'journal of food studies'. In *A Kipper*, first published in 1988, he dispensed wise thoughts and hilarious anecdotes not only on the Giant Mekong Catfish but on the history of the pressure cooker, on nuts, esculent fungi, the artistry of Tokyo's coffee *barista* and much else besides.

The Oxford Companion to Food came towards the end of his writing career. It took twenty years to compile and confirmed his iconic status. Official recognition followed when in 2002 he was awarded the Erasmus Prize. By chance it was on the evening that this award was announced, and when the Davidson house in Chelsea was therefore under siege by European TV crews, that I presented myself for supper. By then I was one of his most ardent fans. I had boated up the Mekong, taken his name in vain, acquired many of his books, and could quote most of *A Kipper*'s 'Giant of the Mekong' essay verbatim. Though this was to be our first and only meeting, I felt we were already friends.

Alan opened the door; Jane switched off the phone. A bottle was produced, although Alan himself neither drank wine nor wrote of it; like *haute cuisine*, it invited too much 'gastronomic gush'. We sat down to roast chicken in the kitchen. Catfish featured only as conversational fare.

It is not true that reading and writing are unsociable activities. Hours spent in the paginated company of a stylish author afford as many insights, present as many challenges and may engender as much affection as years of personal acquaintance. Living and working in the society of authors is like participating in some exotic function without the onus of attendance yet with every chance of a truly life-enriching encounter. When Alan died almost exactly a year later, I felt no great sense of loss. The man I knew lived on in the books. I turned to his essay on 'Funeral Cookbooks' and came up smiling. Try it.

JOHN KEAY's *Mad about the Mekong* was published in February. He and Julia Keay are currently at large in London preparing a new edition of *The London Encyclopaedia*.

The Pick of the Pocket Editions

JOHN SAUMAREZ SMITH

During the early 1970s I read most of Anthony Trollope's novels. This was encouraged by my boss, Handasyde Buchanan, and by an American friend who read them at the same sort of pace and later assembled a wonderful collection of first editions. The novels provided us with infinite hours of pleasure and also introduced us to the perfect reading format for nineteenth-century novels, the World's Classics, published by the Oxford University Press. The original World's Classics were clearly printed on good-quality paper, bound 'in superfine art cloth', and they could be carried anywhere and everywhere in a pocket. They have also become my private litmus test for second-hand bookshops. If I find a couple of shelves, ideally including favourite titles like *The Real Charlotte* or *The Nebuly Coat* or Stanhope's *Conversations with Wellington*, I can be fairly sure that the bookseller is a reader and that his stock is worth investigating. If I find obvious duds – the novels of Constance Holme, say, or odd volumes of *English Critical Essays* – that have probably languished on the same shelf for several years, or if there is no sign at all of the small dark-blue covers, I know I'm probably wasting my time.

For those like me who look out for, and sometimes even retain, useless knowledge, the first World's Classic, published in 1901, was *Jane Eyre*; the last in the original pre-paperback series, published in 1973, was *Crime and Punishment*. The latter was No. 619, making the series many hundred volumes shorter than the original Everyman edition of classics, and many hundreds longer than the modern Everyman which started in 1992. If you had read even half of its remarkable range, you could consider yourself very widely read.

It was the publisher Grant Richards who instigated World's Classics, and Oxford only took over after the first sixty-six titles had appeared and Richards had gone bust. The Everyman series started soon after in 1906 with its first choice of fifty books, edited by Ernest Rhys. In Peter Sutcliffe's informal history of the Oxford University Press, he makes an interesting comparison between these two products of 'the golden age of reading'. World's Classics inclined to be whimsical, 'their small format not compatible with the reverential approach to Great Literature', whereas Everyman 'sought a solemn bond between publisher and reader'. Both series struck a popular chord, and World's Classics helped to establish once and for all that Oxford was a general publisher.

Trollope is responsible for thirty-seven titles in the series: thirty-five novels, *Tales of All Countries* which was called 'First Series' but never achieved a successor, and his vivid *Autobiography*. As committed Trollopians know, this is by no means the full oeuvre and it is interesting that several lesser-known novels like *The Macdermots of Ballycloran* (his first) and *The Bertrams* were published by the Bodley Head in a similar small format during the first years of the last century. In 1907 World's Classics surprisingly chose *The Three Clerks* as their pioneer and, less surprisingly, waited until 1918 before they tried another, *The Warden*. Thereafter, with the enthusiastic support of Humphrey Milford who later became publisher to the Press, novels followed in quick succession, but they never included the Bodley Head titles; presumably Oxford felt that readers would have them already. Even so, this remained the best available run of Trollope until the complete set was published by the Trollope Society and the Folio Society between 1988 and 2000.

My own Trollopes have always lived on the top shelf of a bookcase and my Tolstoys are on another top shelf elsewhere. The Tolstoys were left to me some years ago and date from the 1920s. They still have their original dust wrappers which not only protect them but also provide, on the verso, a list of the volumes of Biography, Essays,

We think of World's Classics in their familiar dark blue binding, but before this became their uniform, the publishers tried a wide variety of bindings and even imprints.

History, Letters, Criticism and Travel published in the series. And in case you miss this, a ten-page list of available titles, with extra information about 'gift bindings', is included at the back of each volume.

The World's Classics' Tolstoys were translated by Aylmer Maude and his wife Louise. In contrast, Turgenev was being translated at the same time by Constance Garnett to appear under the Heinemann imprint in neat, dark green, as opposed to the Oxford blue, volumes. This means that you will only find one Turgenev in World's Classics, *A Nest of Gentlefolk*, and one Chekhov for the same reason: Mrs Garnett had been commissioned by another publisher, Chatto & Windus, to translate his short stories and plays.

The modern reader might speculate on what the Literary Great and Good would now deem to be World's Classics. The original categories were alphabetically listed thus: Anthologies, Autobiography, Biography, The 'Classics', Drama, Essays and Belles Lettres, Fiction, History, Letters, Literary Criticism, Philosophy and Science, Poetry, Politics, Political Economy, Political Theory, Religion, Short Stories, Travel and Topography. Would you guess, even if you'd noticed three titles by Hazlitt in the first twenty-five published books, that, after Fiction, the most popular section was Essays and Belles Lettres?

No category could be labelled 'insular' and the range of short stories, obviously popular with readers who travelled, is remarkably international. The first anthology was *Polish Tales* in 1921, followed by *Persian Legends* two years later. As suitable editors were found for different nationalities, so the collections appeared: Czech and Russian in 1925, Spanish and Austrian in 1928, French in 1932 and German in 1934. There was then a long gap before the first of two volumes of New Zealand stories was published in 1953, followed by two Australian collections, and single volumes devoted to Canadian, Yugoslav, Hungarian, Romanian and American stories, and Icelandic sagas. There were Welsh and Scottish collections too but not, surprisingly, any Irish ones.

The authors who play no part in World's Classics are those like Henry James, Hardy and Kipling whose pocket editions were minting money for Macmillan. *Montrose* was the only John Buchan, and *Ivanhoe* the only Walter Scott, presumably on the grounds that every educated gent had inherited at least one set of the Waverley novels. Nor did anything by Conrad appear until 1940, with *Four Tales*, which was later reprinted as *The Nigger of the Narcissus and Other Tales*. Edith Wharton has only one book in the series, *The House of Mirth*, whereas Mrs Gaskell and George Eliot were published *in toto*.

Twenty-five years ago, Oxford University Press surprisingly decided to sell off its remaining stock of World's Classics at £1 each. If Heywood Hill had had some extra storage space, we should have taken fifty copies of each of our favourite titles. We didn't and I only remember the event because another American friend, more Dickensian than Trollopian, told me that his office was moving to Dallas, Texas, and that he would be needing large numbers of portable books to read while commuting from New York. He bought a copy of every remaindered title (there were well over 200), most of which he has now read. That tribute alone testifies to the taste of the editors over seventy years.

JOHN SAUMAREZ SMITH has been buying and selling old and new books at Heywood Hill for forty years.

A Painterly Eye

NICHOLAS BAGNALL

I first discovered Theodor Storm about eight years ago when someone sent me a copy of *The Dykemaster* in an excellent translation by Denis Jackson. I say excellent, not because of its truth to the original German, of which I'm not competent to judge, but because of its strong and consistently evocative English; like all good translations, it brings its own flavour to the story.

And what a story! Storm wrote it in 1871 and the setting is the coast of North Friesland a century earlier, with the heroic dykemaster's plan to strengthen the sea defences being impeded by the ignorance and prejudice of the locals, as if the forces of man as well as of nature were against him. The historical background is less important, though, than the threatening climate of that storm-tossed coast and the immediate circumstances of its inhabitants' daily existence, intimately described. You're reminded a little of Thomas Hardy, in whose novels the tribulations of Tess or Jude are somehow given an extra-keen edge by our knowledge of the landscapes in which they move.

Since then the same publisher and translator have produced a collection of three of Storm's novellas under the title *Paul the Puppeteer*, which is the English title of the most substantial of the three. This is a much gentler tale than *The Dykemaster*, and much less widely

---

Theodor Storm, *The Dykemaster* (1888) · 156pp · £8.95 · ISBN 0946162549; *Paul the Puppeteer* (1874) with *The Village on the Moor* (1872) and *Renate* (1878) · 156pp · £9.95 · ISBN 0946162700 · Both translated by Denis Jackson and published in paperback by Angel Books.

known, though in its own way equally compelling.

It's set mostly in the same part of the world that Storm knew and understood so well, Friesland, this time in the town of Husum a few miles inland. Its narrator, Paul, is an old craftsman telling the author the story of his life: how a travelling puppet master brings his show to the town, how the boy Paul falls for the puppet master's daughter and how, many years later, in the distant German town of Heiligenstadt, he is able to rescue the innocent father from undeserved imprisonment.

The ending is happy and the whole thing rich in sentiment. Does the child Lisei have beautiful black eyelashes and do they lie modestly on a perfectly formed cheek? They most certainly do, but haven't we seen plenty of such creatures elsewhere? Why, then, does the reader (or this one at any rate) find himself falling as heavily for her as does the infatuated Paul? Why does one bite one's lip with anxiety when Paul breaks the puppet master's best puppet, or when the local yobbos start to wreck the show? And why, when our now grown-up heroine, half-starving, sees Paul's face and cries out his name in the icy town square of Heiligenstadt, does one find one's heart swelling for a moment with relief and joy?

It's Theodor Storm's painterly eye, of course, that does the trick. He takes us to the places where it happens and we see them plain; we are there. One can almost smell the drains. The genre was labelled 'poetic realism' (Storm himself was a poet first and a fiction-writer only second) and it's this deliberate and carefully cultivated realism that gives his narrative its credibility.

It becomes even more important when he is dealing with the supernatural, as he does in *Renate*, another story in this collection. *Paul the Puppeteer* was first seen as a children's story, but *Renate* is grown-up business from the start. He puts it in the form of a recently discovered pastor's journal written in the early eighteenth century, at a time when large numbers of sensible people, including most of the clergy of course, believed in the corporeal existence of the Devil and the power of witchcraft; and indeed its heroine, another beauty, is clearly and alarmingly in thrall to the forces of evil. I can't say I turned the lights up higher as I read it, but the realist technique helped keep disbelief at bay. Storm was a radical and an anticlerical humanist, but his rationalism did not extend to the matter of ghosts. There's an impressive one in *The Dykemaster* that rides on a spectral grey horse and gives you a sinister shudder.

I see that the translator's introduction to *Paul the Puppeteer* also compares Storm's work with Hardy's, for similar reasons. And although Hardy doesn't have much truck with ghosts, he and Theodor Storm do share that knack of conveying a sense not so much of gloom as of unease, a half-formulated knowledge that sooner or later something unnerving is going to happen. The first story in the collection is called *The Village on the Moor* and is perhaps more Hardyesque (if you'll forgive the word) than the others, being concerned with a rich farmer's self-destructive obsession with a local *femme fatale*.

Denis Jackson has more than once been all over the terrain covered in Storm's work, and the new volume has about thirty pages of explanatory notes which, though I suppose not essential to the reader's enjoyment, certainly added to mine.

NICHOLAS BAGNALL, a former literary editor of the *Sunday Telegraph*, was educated at Oxford, where he sat at the feet of J. R. R. Tolkien and acquired a taste for unnerving legends.

No Whingeing!

C. J. DRIVER

I can't remember now the order in which I read them, but I doubt I would have begun with the first of Mary Grant Bruce's novels, just because of its title: *A Little Bush Maid*. It was Billabong itself – the Australian outback station in the north of Victoria, seventeen miles from the nearest settlement – that first caught my imagination and that sent me back to the library in the South African town where I lived to find more of the same:

> [The] country lay bare enough in the early winter – long stretches of stone-walled paddocks where the red soil showed through the sparse native grass; steep, stony hillsides; oases of irrigation, with the deep green of Lucerne growing rank among weed-fringed water channels; and so on and on, past little towns and tiny settlements . . . But Norah did not want the towns; she was homesick for the open country, for the scent of the gum trees coming drifting in through the open window [of the train], for the long, lonely plains . . .

Mary Bruce Grant, *A Little Bush Maid* (1910)

HarperCollins Australia · Pb · 252pp · A$14.95 · ISBN 0207191042

Other titles in the series can be obtained second-hand or through the Internet: *Mates at Billabong* (1911) · *Norah of Billabong* (1913) · *From Billabong to London* (1915) · *Jim and Wally* (1916) · *Captain Jim* (1919) · *Back to Billabong* (1921) ·*Billabong's Daughter* (1924) · *Billabong Adventures* (1927) · *Bill of Billabong* (1931) · *Billabong's Luck* (1933) · *Wings above Billabong* (1935) · *Billabong Gold* (1937) ·*Son of Billabong* (1939) · *Billabong Riders* (1942)

Until I was 9, my mother read aloud to my brother and me every evening – and why bother to read to yourself when someone will do it for you? I could read if I had to, as my father had discovered when he came back from POW camp in Germany and thought he'd better teach me himself. My mother eventually solved the problem by reading a very exciting story to the middle of a chapter, then closing the book abruptly. 'If you want any more, you'll have to read it yourself,' she said. By the time I was 10 I was such a voracious reader that I needed not single novels but series. That was one of the advantages of the Billabong books: there were fifteen of them to search out (and I remember, when I got to the last of them, the same sense of outrage as I was to feel years later when Updike killed off Rabbit with an early heart-attack).

There weren't that many specifically South African novels a youngster could read: *Jock of the Bushveld*, of course, but it was by any standards a bloodthirsty story. Olive Schreiner's *The Story of an African Farm* wasn't regarded as suitable for children. Mainly, there were the English 'standards': *The Wind in the Willows*, *Alice*, *Lorna Doone*, *Gulliver*, *Oliver Twist* and *David Copperfield*, *Swallows and Amazons*; but novels which bore some direct relation to one's own landscape – where if you went into a thicket you might as well meet a snake as an elf – were rare. Of course, in one sense northern Victoria was as foreign as the Lake District, but at least an Australian Christmas was stinking hot, not snowy.

A Little Bush Maid began as a serial, from newspaper articles which Minnie (as she was christened) Grant Bruce – a jobbing journalist in Melbourne – had contributed to the children's page she edited. Popular demand made her editor suggest they might make a book. Though it still seems thinly episodic, it does introduce the main cast of characters: David Linton, the owner of Billabong, who had turned 'in a night from a young man to an old one' when his wife died; Norah herself, a tomboy and apple of her father's eye; her big brother, Jim, away at boarding-school some of the time, an athlete and no

intellectual, but straight as a die; Wally Meadows his mate, dark and cheerful, 'a wag of a boy . . . [who] straightaway laid his boyish heart down at Norah's feet, and was her slave from the first day they met'; Mrs Brown, the cook, 'fat, good-natured and adoring'; black Billy, the stable-hand, whose command of English is limited to the word 'plenty'; Mr Hogg the gardener; his sworn enemy, Lee Wing, the Chinese vegetable gardener (complete with queue, or pigtail); Mr Groom, the English storekeeper, who tries to teach Norah to play the piano by more than just ear; Murty O'Toole, head stockman; Dave Boone, one of the station-hands; Sarah and Mary, Irish housemaids; and of course the dogs and the horses, particularly Norah's pony, Bobs. At the centre of the plot is the Hermit, whom Norah befriends and who turns out to be David Linton's long-lost friend, an accountant wrongly accused of dishonesty, who as a consequence had faked his own death before hiding away in the bush.

Mates at Billabong is technically a much fuller and more coherent novel. There are a series of set-pieces, vividly typical of their place and time: the Billabong dance; Christmas celebrations; the cricket-match, Cunjee v. Mulgoa. The plot, however, centres on Cecil, a small, dapper, beautifully dressed cousin, who comes to Billabong to recuperate. Unusually, the country does not reform the lad from the city, and Cecil leaves much as he came, a selfish drip and a coward. Mary Grant Bruce's liberal sympathies are shown in her treatment of two Indian hawkers, Ram Das and Lal Chunder (that name obviously hadn't then taken on the connotation which Barry Humphries was later to popularize, if that's the right word). Mary the housemaid, who has been alarmed by Lal Chunder, actually says of him, 'It's my belief he'd kill us all in our beds as soon as wink! Scarin' the wits out of one with his pink top-knot arrangement – such a thing for a man to wear! Gimme white Orstalia!' Norah laughs at her, and it transpires that Lal Chunder is the hero who, in return for her kindness to him, later saves Norah from an evil swagman, intent on theft and probably more than that.

These are not soft books: the landscape may be hauntingly beautiful, but there are snakes, bush-fires, thunderstorms, criminals on the run. The Hermit nearly dies of typhus; David Linton breaks a leg when he is thrown from his horse in the bush; Norah's pony Bobs breaks his back in a fall; and Norah herself risks her life in a bush-fire to save her father's prize sheep. The value-system is much the same as that of the Australian balladeers such as 'Banjo' Paterson and Henry Lawson: one works hard, plays hard, doesn't whinge, sticks by one's mates, doesn't show off, doesn't care much about ideas, keeps emotion to oneself, does what one has to do because that's what one does, and judges people by what they do, not what they say or (most of all) what they are. The writing is surprisingly unmawkish: the sentiment is in the situation, not in the words.

I am glad to find *A Little Bush Maid* is still in print, though I suspect it might seem as dated to the present-day young as do illustrations (mainly by J. Macfarlane) of youngsters riding in jackets, collars and ties. I wouldn't want to put the Billabong books in the pantheon of great children's literature, but they still bear joyful rereading, more than fifty years after I first read them.

C. J. DRIVER was for more than twenty years a headmaster, but is now once again a full-time writer. He has published six books of poetry. His fifth novel, *Shades of Darkness*, was published by Jonathan Ball (Johannesburg and Cape Town) last year – and a sixth is now complete and in need of a publisher.

The Book Hound

Slightly Foxed's Book Hound has run to earth a selection of interesting new fiction which may well get lost behind the piles of bestsellers.

Stuart McLean • *Home from the Vinyl Café: A Year of Stories*

Dave runs a downtown Toronto record store (motto: 'We may not be big, but we're small'). Morley, his wife, runs their house, two kids and a variety of pets. Their lives revolve like the stylus on an old '45, always meeting in the middle – eventually. In a succession of stories as funny as anything I've read in years McLean creates a domestic portrait that is by turns honest, painful and worryingly close to home. Dave's attempt to disguise the fact that he has forgotten to buy the Christmas turkey had me choking with laughter over my cup of tea.

Granta · Pb · 272pp · £9.99 · ISBN 1862077746

Kat Pomfret • *Paradise Jazz*

Pomfret's debut novel appears, at first glance, to be a successor to Zadie Smith's *White Teeth*. It is the story of two girls, one white, one black, both with their own reasons for wanting to discover more about their past. Helena has lost both parents to cancer within a year of each other and now, more than ever, needs to understand her roots. Georgetown would settle for knowing the identity of her father and why she was named for an American suburb she has never visited. Their narratives intertwine in a novel flavoured with jazz and fried chicken. As I followed them from the Deep South of the USA to the grey sprawl of '90s London, I genuinely felt I was witnessing the start of a fine literary career.

Snowbooks · Pb · 428pp · £6.99 · ISBN 1905005083

Cat Weatherill • *Barkbelly*

This is the most inventive and delightful story for any age that I am likely to read all year. Barkbelly is a wooden boy who has fallen from the sky, naturally enough, as a wooden egg. Raised by Gable Gantry (on whose head he first landed) and his wife Pumpkin, he is slowly accepted by the people of Pumbleditch. That is, until an inevitable and tragic accident forces him to flee in fear. What follows is an epic journey, sparkling with a cast of characters that never fails to delight, amuse, scare or dumbfound as required. This is a truly magical tale which will inspire children and make adults wish they were kids again – a classic in the making.

Puffin · Pb · 340pp · £9.99 · ISBN 0141381167

Tom Perrotta • *Little Children*

British publishers seem to be scared of the American writer Tom Perrotta. Though he has written some of the funniest and best-observed novels of the past ten years (including the excellent *Election* which was turned into an equally unsung film), until now no one has published his books in the UK. Full marks, therefore, to Allison & Busby who have been brave enough to give him a go. *Little Children* is the literary equivalent of a cross between *American Beauty*, *Desperate Housewives* and *Six Feet Under* – witty, subversive and very clever.

Allison & Busby · Hb · 356pp · £12.99 · ISBN 0749083042

The Editor Regrets

DEREK PARKER

Suddenly, out of the blue, one morning in December 1965, a letter arrived on the delightfully old-fashioned headed notepaper of the Poetry Society ('Patron, Sir Compton Mackenzie, LL.D., F.R.S.L., President, Professor Nevill Coghill, M.A., F.R.S.L.'), written, but not signed, by Robert Armstrong, Secretary and Treasurer.

John Smith, it said, had decided that a four-year stint as Editor of the *Poetry Review* was 'about enough'. He and Armstrong had undertaken 'an intimate review' of the situation, and were now writing to ask whether I might care to take on the job.

I think it was John – a poet and literary agent – who had actually put my name forward. I'd corresponded with him for about fifteen years, first from Cornwall as an admirer of his poetry, and had known him personally in London for five or six; we had much the same view of contemporary poets and poetry, and I suppose it wasn't altogether surprising that he suggested me.

It would, I thought, be rather interesting to see what I could do with the *Review*. I'd seen it, off and on, since the mid-'50s. It was published by the Poetry Society and supported by the money they raised from their examinations in verse-speaking. These had been set up, or at least the basic textbook in verse-speaking had been written, by Wallace Nichols, himself a bad stammerer who nevertheless spoke verse impeccably (and wearing another hat wrote the adventures of a Roman slave detective for the *London Mystery Magazine*). Wallace lived just outside Penzance in the Elizabethan wing of a mansion occupied by His Honour Judge Scobell Armstrong, an eccentric who once ordered the defendant in a court case to pay costs in frogs.

I'd begun occasionally to contribute poems and reviews myself, which were sympathetically accepted by John. But editing it? I didn't hesitate nearly long enough. I didn't realize, for instance, that the then Council of the Poetry Society looked on the magazine as a private journal for members, and incidentally as an outlet for their own poetry, for most of them were poets – with the exception of the admirable chairman, Mrs Hester Marsden-Smedley, sometime Mayor of Chelsea, who presided at meetings and at lectures, often happily slipping into unconsciousness after introducing the speaker. I remember John Betjeman being particularly amused to see her snoring gently through a reading of *Summoned by Bells*.

I don't think John Smith ever made a really firm attempt to change the conception of the magazine as basically a platform for the Society's members – though perhaps he did, and the reaction was one of the reasons why he decided he had had 'about enough', because the Council, and even more the General Secretary, were not amused when I tried to do so.

Robert Armstrong was an accountant but was devoted to what I suspect he may have called 'poesy'. Fifteen years earlier, Muriel Spark had edited the *Review*, and I was amused to read in her autobiography, when it came out, that he had been a major irritant in her life. The trouble was that he really wanted to edit the magazine himself, or at least to ensure from a distance that it only contained work by his friends and/or himself. He never actually confronted me, but even when he ceased to be Secretary he caused endless trouble with the Council, who seemed to have been given the assurance that anything they sent me would be published without question.

In those days, despite John's best endeavours, the *Review* was pretty much a joke with professional poets and critics, and it was generally known that one of the easiest ways of making Geoffrey Grigson laugh (and they weren't legion) was to mention the magazine. Would it be possible to change that? Well, one way, I thought, would be to get a few reputable names together. So I wrote to a few poets I knew, and many I didn't, and among the contributors to my first two issues (Spring and Summer, 1966) were – in no particular order – Charles Causley, Roy Fuller, Vernon Watkins, Anna Akhmatova, Thom Gunn, William Plomer, Elizabeth Jennings, John Heath-Stubbs, Adrian Mitchell, Ted Walker and Vernon Scannell.

None of these, I should point out, had ever submitted poems before. I don't think it would have occurred to them. However, it had occurred to a lot of other poets, if 'poets' is the word I seek. John Smith had not told me how many unsolicited manuscripts he had had to deal with. The problem was that the *Poetry Review* was then the only periodical listed in the *Writers' and Artists' Yearbook* with the word 'poetry' in the title, so anyone with a piece of verse lying about the house almost automatically sent it off to the office in Earls Court, and twice a week I would collect a number of large buff envelopes containing about 250 other envelopes, each concealing a clutch of what someone thought of as poems.

Sometimes, of course, they really were poems. I did 'discover' – though really of course they had discovered themselves; all I did was recognize them – a number of fine poets, some of whom have subsequently made reputations, and some not. I remember with pleasure coming across the work of Ted Walker, Edward Lucie-Smith, Thomas Blackburn, Harry Guest, Tully Potter . . . and indeed Seamus Heaney, who had just published his first collection, *Eleven Poems*. I'd never heard the name or read the poems, but the ones he sent leaped off the page with unmistakable life and spirit.

I'd never been backward, as an ordinary reader, in claiming to recognize a good poem when I saw it, but reading or at least looking at almost a thousand a week severely damaged my conviction. An immediate reaction of 'rubbish' was all too often followed by the thought that perhaps, after all, it wasn't. I went through several weeks of self-doubt. But then I mentioned this to George MacBeth, who at that time was editing a BBC Radio poetry magazine.

'Well,' he said, 'all you can do is print what you like.' That helped a lot – though it sometimes led to trouble. I fought a bitter battle with Armstrong, for instance, about turning over almost an entire issue to a very long poem entitled 'Ichor', by Gavin Bantock. In the end, I invoked the aid of Nevill Coghill, who fortunately also admired the poem and wrote a Foreword to the issue praising it and claiming that it was 'happy for us that our new editor is a man of risks and discoveries'. Well, yes and no. The reaction of almost everybody else was negative – and I have to say I think everybody else was probably right.

Ploughing through the buff envelopes was a mixed pleasure. Admittedly, most could be stuffed back in the enclosed stamped addressed envelope without too much compunction. Occasionally, it was worth scribbling on the rejection slip something condescending like: 'Not quite – but please do send something more when you have it.' Always a mistake – one invariably got, by return of post, a larger envelope containing 35 more poems.

There was, however, the very real pleasure of the thoroughly bad poem – the poem that the editors would without question have published in *The Stuffed Owl* had they had the joy of reading it. One of my favourites was the 'Ode to a Sweat Gland', by E. F. St John Lyburn, who must have been a doctor. His poem was not just a fancy, it was a practical essay:

> You should wrap in a plastic and sweat the whole day.
> This will stop the blood clotting, this really will pay.
> The cause is thrombosis, you may get it again.
> The blood is now thinner as a wet sweat is sane.
> So a tip to you all is to stop this sad plight
> For virtue is knowledge, and to sweat is a right.

There was much, much more. Antonio Carmentine was more laconic, more romantic, more in touch with nature and the seasons, which he welcomed with a joyous trill:

Spring is a welcome season,
As we all know the reason,
For the snows and ice have finally melted
And the animals no longer need to be shelted . . .

while

Winter is a time which all will remember,
Which usually occurs in early November,
When the glorious summer heat
Has vanished in endless retreat,
Leaving behind a thick carpet of dazzling white snow
Which in turn will have to go.

Carmentine's prosody, I thought, might have been envied by the immortal William McGonagall. Prosody wasn't – I'm sure isn't – a strong point with most amateur poets. Alan Gardner, for instance, was passionate about music, but his rhythms were not perhaps as light and flexible as those of his favourite composers:

Now Beethoven wrote sweet music
While the works of Bach are rather sad,
George Bizet gave us opera,
And Brahms's songs are sometimes glad . . .
Wolfgang Mozart surpassed all others
And deserves a fuller account of his fame;
In six weeks he wrote his three brilliant symphonies,
E flat, G minor and C are their names.

Bad poetry has an irresistible charm, especially when it can be described as 'thoroughly well-meaning', like the 'Ode Dedicated to James Gibb on his Retirement as the Fraserburgh Golf Club Professional in 1969'. But I must confess to feeling slightly guilty for smiling at such poems, however sympathetically. Some of course are almost impossible to smile at; the tragedy of Aberfan brought out a number of them. In what is on the whole a non-poetry-reading country, it is surprising how many people try to express themselves in verse (I bet my successor at what is now a first-rate magazine was deluged with bad verse after the death of Princess Diana).

I battled on with the *Review* for five years. They got me cheap. I was allowed, I think, to claim for necessary postage, on production of a post office receipt, but though the poets were (properly) paid, I wasn't. However, I had the last laugh. Just after I handed over the job to some other patron of the art, I nearly threw away the correspondence file I'd kept – the Society had no room for it, they said – but then I decided to hand it over to a bookseller who specialized in selling MSS. To my astonishment (most of the stuff amounted only to 'Nothing for you at the moment, I'm afraid – W. H. Auden' or 'Sorry for the bad handwriting – Stevie Smith') he was able to sell the collection to an American university library for £1,000 – the deposit on a mortgage for a little cottage in Cambridge. Maybe I should have called it Poets' Corner. But I didn't.

DEREK PARKER later edited *The Author* for eighteen years; he now lives in Sydney. His biography of Voltaire was published in January, and he has just completed a biography of the Countess of Strathmore, great-great-great-great-grandmother of the Queen, to be published next year.

Coming attractions . . .

PENELOPE LIVELY explores the genius of William Golding

SIMON BRETT casts a fresh eye on Gwen Raverat

WILLIAM PALMER blows Louis Armstrong's trumpet

KATE DUNN remembers the Puffin Club

DEREK ROBINSON rewrites his CV

PAUL ROUTLEDGE makes Eastern approaches

PETER SWAAB goes to the Vatican

ANNABEL WALKER stays on

Bibliography

James Baldwin, *Giovanni's Room* 42

Mary Grant Bruce, *A Little Bush Maid* 79

Alan Davidson, *Fish and Fish Dishes of Laos; A Kipper with My Tea* 67

Roger Deakin, *Waterlog* 7

Ian and Jennifer Glynn, *The Life and Death of Smallpox* 37

Aidan Hartley, *The Zanzibar Chest* 11

C.L.R. James, *Beyond a Boundary* 46

Captain W. E. Johns, The Biggles books 19

Tobias Jones, *The Dark Heart of Italy* 11

Ghada Karmi, *In Search of Fatima* 11

John W. Kiser, *The Monks of Tibhirine* 11

Stuart McLean, *Home from the Vinyl Café: A Year of Stories* 83

William H. McNeill, *Plagues and Peoples* 37

Tom Perrotta, *Little Children* 84

Kat Pomfret, *Paradise Jazz* 83

Gaylord Schanilec, *Mayflies of the Driftless Region* 50

Deborah Scroggins, *Emma's War* 11

Wallace Stegner, *Angle of Repose* 56

Theodor Storm, *The Dykemaster; Paul the Puppeteer* 76

David Thomson, *Woodbrook* 25

Ethel Lillian Voynich, *The Gadfly* 60

Cat Weatherill, *Barkbelly* 84

Stefan Zweig, *Beware of Pity; Casanova; Confusion; The Invisible Collection & Buchmendel; The Royal Game; Twenty-four Hours in the Life of a Woman* 31